WHAT PRICE
FOR
BLOOD?

MURDER AND JUSTICE
IN SAUDI ARABIA

Robert J. Meadows, Ph.D.

Robert D. Reed Publishers
San Francisco

ISBN 1-885003-31-5

Library of Congress Catalog Card No. 99-066905

Cover design by Irene Taylor, it grafx
Typesetting by Barbara Kruger

Robert D. Reed Publishers
San Francisco

CONTENTS

ACKNOWLEDGMENTS

I undertook the challenge of writing this book for two reasons. First, I wanted to acquaint the reader with the culture of Saudi Arabia. It became clear when I started writing that there is a great deal of ignorance and misunderstanding about Islamic justice in the West, particularly as applied in Saudi Arabia. Without doubt, it is a system of which Westerners have little understanding, but quickly condemn. Second, the tragic murder of Australian nurse, Yvonne Gilford, is an engaging precedent-setting case because for the first time a challenge was launched against the Saudi confessional justice process.

This book is a revealing glimpse of Muslim culture, crime and justice. Due to the support provided by the Saudi Arabian law firm of Salah Al-Hejailan, the information collected for this book is also precedent setting. I know of no other case where a humble Western academician like myself has been permitted access to the criminal legal files of a Saudi Arabian law firm. I am privileged, honored, and lucky, to say the least. As a consequence, I am sure that no other book on this case will have the breadth or quality of information as this one.

Numerous hours of research and writing, with many contributing their time and efforts, went into the production of this book. In addition to researching various sources about Islam and Saudi Arabia, I was provided case information and conducted interviews with persons familiar with the case. First and foremost, I wish to thank the Saudi Arabian law firm of Salah Al-Hejailan. Mr. Hejailan and his associates, Michael Dark and Robert Thoms, provided valuable information and insight. Without the cooperation of Mr. Hejailan and his firm, this book would not be possible. I want to thank Sultan Hejailan, a student and friend, for assisting me in developing ideas for the book, and for interpreting and transcribing Arabic legal documents. Fares Hejailan, a student at the school of African and Oriental studies in London, provided critical comment and suggestions on Islamic law. I wish to thank Jonathan Ashbee, Deborah Parry's brother-in-law, who made over a dozen trips to Saudi Arabia, for providing crucial information regarding Deborah Parry and Saudi justice. Rodger Pannone, one of the key lawyers in the case, provided additional understanding into the delicate negotiations leading to the release of the nurses. My sincere thanks to Ms. Kim Anklin and California Lutheran University student Jennifer Ware, who assisted with the research and writing. My appreciation to Dr. Paul Hanson, Professor of History at California Lutheran

University, Fred Tonsing, Professor of Religion at California Lutheran University, Peggy Johnson, University Relations, and Lynda Paige Fulford (Lè Brat), Director of Public Information and University Relations at California Lutheran University, for providing helpful editorial comments.

PROLOGUE

In the early morning hours of December 12, 1996, the bloodied body of Yvonne Gilford was discovered in her bedroom at the King Fahd Military Medical Complex, located Dhahran, Saudi Arabia. The 55-year-old Australian nurse working for the Saudi National Ministry of Health was repeatedly stabbed, bludgeoned, and suffocated, implying a passion killing, or a murder committed out of extreme anger. Speculation quickly arose that the deed may have been the work of a criminal sociopath knowledgeable about the victim, her lifestyle, and general layout of the compound. Yet the crime was not just a malicious killing marred in hate: it was a message. Every slicing stab wound and blow was an inadvertent signature left by an angry person. Several days after the murder, roommates Lucille McLauchlan and Deborah Parry, British nurses working at the same hospital, were arrested for the murder. The two nurses were subsequently charged, Parry with murder and McLauchlan as an accessory to murder.

The outcry in 1997 over the fate of the two nurses presented Britain's Labor government with its first diplomatic crisis since coming to power. Saudi Arabia, after all, is one of Britain's major trading partners with, at the time of the murder, a pending arms-for-oil deal worth an estimated $32 billion.

The Saudi police accused Parry, with McLauchlan's assistance, of attacking Gilford after ending an intense lesbian affair. Testimony offered by independent witnesses indicated that on the evening before the murder, the three expatriates were observed arguing at a party. While in police custody, the nurses confessed to the killing. The nurses subsequently retracted their statements declaring the Saudi police orchestrated the confessions as the result of torture and threats of physical and sexual abuse. No witnesses surfaced nor was any forensic evidence presented at the nearly year-long trial. From the Saudi perspective, the case hinged primarily on the nurses' retracted confessions (although there was circumstantial evidence to boot).

A number of "who done it" theories hovered over the compound after the nurses' arrest. One of the nurses' lawyers suggested that the murder might have been committed by a security guard responsible for patrolling the residential complex. The week before Yvonne Gilford's murder, she had been the subject of unsolicited attention by a guard. A bracelet found in the room of the deceased after the murder was one customarily worn by a man. It was rumored Gilford operated a loan-sharking business out of the compound, which created a lot of enemies. Could it be that a security guard or intruder other than the named defendants committed the ghastly murder over a loan-sharking deal? Although never solved, a similar type of murder had occurred at the hospital in 1994.

The nurses were tried under Islamic law, resulting in Parry's murder conviction with possible execution by beheading. Under the Islamic concept of kisas, punishment should be proportionate to the wrongful act; thus, a murder conviction carries the possible imposition of the death penalty. For her part in the crime, McLauchlan was sentenced to eight years imprisonment and 500 lashes. Parry, confronted with the unpleasant possibility of losing her head, and McLauchlan, facing imprisonment and a severe whipping, sought legal defense from one of the Kingdom's most preeminent lawyers, Salah Al-Hejailan. The esteemed Hejailan, an advisor to the Saudi government with a wealth of legal savvy, worked pro bono. The work of his firm in the case was unprecedented in Saudi jurisprudence in that lawyers representing criminal defendants normally do not appear in court.

Under the Islamic law, known as Sharia law, and in cases of intentional murder, the murdered victim's immediate family is entitled to demand execution, forgive the offender, or accept diyah or "blood money." Hejailan and his team of seasoned lawyers crafted a defense and negotiated a monetary settlement with Gilford's family. After a year of bitter and exhausting negotiations, the victim's brother, Frank Gilford, ultimately agreed to accept 1.2 million dollars in blood money.

This acceptance guaranteed Parry would not be executed. British companies raised the money on behalf of the defendants in an effort to keep trade relations between the two countries intact. During the protracted process, the nurses remained in prison, where they suffered from physical ailments and depression. The nurses complained of abuse and torture at the hands of prison authorities. As expected, the crime captured media and public attention in Great Britain, Australia, and the United States.

Compounding the issue was that neither of the nurses' home countries, Great Britain nor Australia, has the death penalty. Additional political implications between Britain and Saudi Arabia prompted King Fahd to commute the nurses' sentences to time served. The King's decision allowed the nurses to return to their native soil. However, the reduction of sentence is not an admission of innocence or a pardon. The nurses are forever guilty under Saudi law.

After release, McLauchlan returned to her native Scotland, selling her story for a reported $100,000. However, upon her return, she faced criminal charges and was convicted in December 1998 of stealing $2,500 from a dying AIDS patient prior to her 1996 exodus to Saudi Arabia. Just before her conviction, her book, Trial by Ordeal, was published. The book is an account of her experiences with Saudi justice and prison.

Deborah Parry cashed in as well by selling her version of the story to the London Daily Express for a reported $100,200. Both nurses continue to deny any involvement with the murder and are critical of their treatment by Saudi authorities. Meanwhile, Frank Gilford, has been widely criticized for accepting the blood money for his sister's death, although about 700,000 pounds was earmarked for the Women's and Children's Hospital in Adelaide, Australia.

A timeline of events is presented in appendix A.

1
SUSPICION AND BLAME

It was a scorching Friday afternoon as two condemned prisoners walked slowly toward the middle of the shopping plaza. The sobbing prisoners wore white robes; their hands manacled behind their backs with their heads tightly covered. Two policemen led the male prisoner, convicted of killing his friend, into the center of the plaza first. Two female officers followed with the condemned woman convicted of killing her husband. The executioner, a large muscular man wearing a white robe and carrying a 4-foot-long crescent-shaped sword, stood by expressionless, patiently waiting to perform his grim duty as he had done so many times before.

First, the condemned man was made to kneel down on the ground, his head over a metal grate, which covered a drain hole. The executioner pulled back the clothing from the man's neck, exposing the skin, leaving his head covered. He poked the man's spine forcing him to arch his back, and with one swift motion, swung the weighty sword, severing the head. The body toppled forward and the head rolled onto the grate, blood spurting from the lifeless torso. The woman met the same disastrous fate. The bodies were quickly removed and the marbled plaza floor immediately cleansed of the blood. The curious, but reserved crowd soon dispersed and business in the plaza went on as usual.

Intentional or premeditated murder in Saudi Arabia is a crime against the family, a private matter, with the family of the deceased assuming the role of prosecutors as to whether the convicted should live or die by the sword. Intentional murder is one committed with malice, the result of planning, or the aftermath of a serious crime such as rape or robbery.

Those condemned face a public execution, usually by beheading, which normally takes place on Friday, a holy day. Death by public beheading is common in the Kingdom, designed to teach or deter others with evil intents. Without doubt, Saudi Arabia applies strict sanctions for those convicted of drug trafficking, murder and rape.

Those convicted of aggravated crimes such as serial killings or multiple murders are administrated a more painful execution. In such cases, the skilled swordsman hits the back of the neck three times without completely chopping off the head. Some degenerate souls may be crucified for 24 hours as an example and deterrent. In 1993, two Saudi Arabian nationals and an Egyptian were executed and crucified in the city of Haql for raping and murdering a woman, her husband and four children

In cases of murder, death does not always follow for convicted murderers. In lieu of death, Islamic law allows the victim's family to forgive the offender, or accept "blood money" known as Diya. It is an offering by the convicted person, or his family, in exchange for life. The traditional amount of blood money in Saudi Arabia is either 100 camels, 200 cows, 1,000 sheep, or a cash equivalent. If the victim is a woman, the sum is halved. Blood money does not mean unconditional freedom, for the government can still impose public justice such as prison for those lucky enough to escape the grasp of the grim reaper.

As expected, the 1996 brutal murder of Australian nurse Yvonne Gilford created international attention and unwelcome scrutiny of the Saudi justice system. It is the type of crime that isn't supposed to happen in western compounds, especially in a nation with strict laws and punishments. The case is about crime, justice, and punishment in a conservative religious culture. But it also became a trial of the Saudi legal process, not just a crime involving a trio of expatriate women embroiled in a dispute. In another respect, the case gives us the opportunity to learn about the role of religion, for it is religion that influences government practices, defining the legal and social mores of this highly prosperous desert nation.

From the beginning, the case prompted criticism from British foreign secretary Robin Cook, who termed Saudi justice "barbaric," resulting in a "clash of cultures" between the two countries. Indeed, the case is about conflicting cultures and how justice is administered in the oil-rich Kingdom. In any society, justice is a direct reflection of government philosophy or religious foundations.

History is replete with examples of justice applied in the name of religion, cultural preservation, or ethnic cleansing. Recent events such as the turmoil in Yugoslavia and East Timor Indonesia remind us of how culture, religion, or ones twisted political philosophy define justice.

As the Gilford case progressed, insults and cultural bashing dominated the media. Whether or not any of these attacks caused serious wounds or have any concrete basis is up for debate. The media has a way of reporting events in inflammatory terms; however true or untrue these attacks, both defenders and critics of Islamic justice and culture came out of the closet to offer opinions.

Chris Talbot, a writer for the organization "The Socialist Equality Party of England" wrote an article criticizing the Saudi royal family and the treatment of foreign workers. The English political activist group first entered the Saudi-bashing contest by condemning the alleged brutal treatment inflicted by the Saudi regime on the two nurses while in confinement.

At the time the article was written, October 11, 1997, this organization believed there was no doubt the nurses were denied basic human rights and that their conviction for the murder of Yvonne Gilford was based on confessions extracted under torture.

British irritation over the case parallels another case involving a British national. About the same time the Gilford case was making headlines in 1997, the murder conviction of a 19-year-old British au pair in the United States unleashed a wave of shock and disbelief in Britain, along with fairly widespread condemnation of the American judicial system. In this case, as in the Gilford case, the administration of justice by a foreign nation was scrutinized and condemned.

The alleged murder of an 8-month-old boy by British au pair Louise Woodward was shrouded in controversy and heated debate. Police said that on the 4th of February, 1997, the au pair teenager, frustrated by a curfew set by the infant's parents, shook the baby to death, and at one point slammed his head on a hard surface with enough force to crack his skull, injuring his brain.

The case rested entirely on whether Woodward intentionally killed Matthew Eapen. Like the Gilford case, there were no witnesses, just a lot of circumstantial evidence. But unlike the nurses' case, the trial was public. According to the prosecution, Woodward shook the boy vigorously and slammed him onto a hard surface, causing fatal injuries. The defense brought in experts from around the United States who refuted all this, declaring that Matthew died as a result of a previous unnoticed injury (evidence of scar tissue in the area of the head injury was found), and suffered from a re-bleeding of the wound. In spite of this revelation, the au pair was tried and convicted of second-degree murder to the shock of many, especially the young teen.

The jury could not consider a manslaughter charge because the au pair's defense team, with her approval, persuaded the judge to allow the jury to convict only on first or second-degree murder; a bold legal move that backfired. In American justice, the type of instruction given by the judge to the jury guides their decision or boundaries. Many believed the evidence against the au pair was insufficient to convict for murder. Nonetheless, Woodward was sent to prison. On appeal, her sentence (much to the amazement of many) was reduced to manslaughter, a lesser form of murder. This reduction allowed her to be set free after serving only a year of her prison sentence. The decision stirred anger and applause from both sides of the pond, dividing legal experts and the public alike.

As with the au pair case, the Saudi case inflamed passions and inspired steaming debates of justice. But the murder of Yvonne Gilford was special as well as troubling. The murder took place in a land with no direct media coverage. Investigative reporting is unprecedented in Saudi Arabia and the government was not about to make an exception.

Ignorance and secrecy shrouded the case because the Saudis are reluctant to publicize cases inviting criticism of their judicial system; such attacks can also be construed to be an attack on their culture. In other words, the Saudi's are constantly blamed by such groups as England based Amnesty International for alleged human rights violations. While a cloud of media attention and criticism loomed over the Saudi justice process, a poll of the average British citizen presented a different picture. Not all British citizens were fans of the nurses and some sided with the Saudi version of events.

In September, 1997, a popular British talk radio show discussed the case for over four hours. The show, hosted by James Whale, broadcast live from 9 p.m. until 1 a.m., boasted the highest listening audience of any national evening show. During the program, listeners offered opinions about the conviction of the two nurses and the Saudi style of justice, and remarkably, over 60 percent of the callers supported Saudi Arabia's stance.

There are journalists who felt no compassion for the nurses' unfortunate predicament. Some argued that whatever was awaiting them was their own fault, not the Saudis'. They, and no one else, chose to live, work, and play in a foreign land with vastly different rules. The nurses knew the rules, screwed up, got caught and were crying foul.

Irish writer Kevin Myers best summed up their plight. In his October, 1997 Irish Times commentary titled "Irishman's Diary," Myers is not particularly sympathetic to the nurses' dilemma and, like the polls, believed the Saudis were not entirely to blame, if at all, for this calamitous scenario.

Irishman's Diary
The article in this newspaper last Saturday by the Guardian journalist Kathy Evans about the two British nurses sentenced for the murder of

an Australian nurse provided an interesting insight into journalistic standards. It is the first time that I have read of two convicted murderers (found guilty by a Saudi preliminary court) being referred to by first name, as if the article were in a girls' school magazine.

In the vast body of material written about this case, the most invisible person of all is the murdered Australian, whose death appears to be an inconvenient obstacle in the way of an entirely virtuous frenzy about Saudi justice. To remind you: this woman was beaten, knifed and suffocated to death in her flat. The two women held by the Saudi authorities were found using her bankcards. All three were nurses together in the men's renal unit of the King Fahd Military Medical Complex in Dhahran. The allegation is that the two British women—Deborah Parry and Lucille McLauchlan—had a fight with the Australian, Yvonne Gilford (who was having an affair with Parry), and, in the heat of the moment, stabbed, beat and suffocated her.

Tones of indignation

The two women were interrogated, during which they later said they were sexually molested and were threatened, before they confessed, without recourse to defense counsel. This has been reported in Britain and Ireland in barely suppressed tones of indignation, as if nobody is ever threatened or compelled to confess (without counsel) to crimes they did not commit in either jurisdiction. Let the words Kelly, Guildford, Birmingham, Bridgewater linger in your ears, if you please. It is true that the nature of the evidence, the privacy in which it is heard, the use of blood money in atonement to the family of the victim, and the truly astonishing punishments inflicted on those found guilty are unique to the Saudi system of justice. Barbarous, we all agree. Public beheading and the lash—such as faced by the two nurses—should remain where they belong, in the Middle Ages. Good. The last lawful public beheading in Europe occurred before thousands of spectators in Paris in 1939, well within the lifetime of the present Saudi king. The last beheading in Europe was in France in 1977, and the victim then was an Arab, Hamida Djandoubi. And last June we passed—though nobody noticed—the 25th anniversary of the last legal flogging in Britain. So much for the superiority of European judicial and penal culture over that of the Arabs. Now, I do not know whether either of the two British nurses is guilty or innocent, though I am aware that an Australian nurse is dead. Had the victim been British, and the alleged killer a Saudi male, I doubt very much whether we would have heard quite so much about the poor accused and the ordeal he had gone through, and rather more about the victim; and we would have heard nothing whatever about the deficiencies in Saudi justice.

Bartered their rights

What is actually far more relevant is that all three women bartered their ordinary human rights to work in Saudi Arabia. They did this knowingly and freely, just as TT racers embark upon their mad, life-shortening circuits of the motorcycle track freely, for fun, adventure and money. You take your risks... As the Saudi ambassador to London, Lujain Al-Iman, recently wrote: "Every guestworker who is accepted for a job in Saudi Arabia is well apprised of its laws and customs before he or she goes, and so must be prepared to live them. British citizens would expect no less of those who live and work [in Britain] as guests." The three women (and their hundreds of Irish co-workers) went to a country which so far this year (with three months still to go) has executed 110 people. Western workers in Saudi Arabia become volunteer-accomplices to the regime, which uses the executioner's sword as an instrument of state. They make a great deal of money by choosing to live and work in a country which beheads and behands (for the most part) native males—who did not choose to live there—and which radically circumcises all native women—who also did not choose to live there—so that they are almost without sexual sensation. Saudi women are transformed into vessels in which men can relieve themselves; and nurses who go there become auxiliaries to a medical system in which the sexual mutilation of girls is universal. The nurses do it freely and for money. The girls do not. There is no obvious way out of the dilemma set by the West's closest friend in the Arab world. Islam and democracy are incompatible. Islam does not even begin to perceive the legitimacy of the secular state with secular law. And, disagreeable though Saudi law might be to us, we might remember that the main opposition in Saudi does not come from pro-democrats but from Islamic fundamentalists who regard the Saudi regime as being wimpish and effete, and who look to the sterling, manly example being set by their coreligionists in Iran, Afghanistan and Algeria.

Powerhouse of capitalism

Happily, no Irish nurses face public execution in Chop Square, or we might face excruciatingly embarrassing demands for a boycott of Saudi goods. The Saudis wouldn't notice. We would. We sell about £150 million worth of goods to them; they sell just £2 million to us. And that is part of the problem. Saudi Arabia is the powerhouse of capitalism upon which the prosperity of the world—not just the multinational oil companies—depends. It is a truly bizarre society whose norms—including the sacerdotal use of the blade and the ritual removal of human flesh—are beyond our understanding. But nobody is obliged to go there. Nobody absolutely has to submit to the vagaries of Saudi law. And nobody is compelled to break those laws once they get there. My sympathy for the maimed or even dead TT motorcyclist is limited: he made his choice; and ditto the Western guest-workers of Saudi.

Whenever any foreign national is tried and convicted of a crime by a host country, particularly Westerners, media attention will undoubtedly accompany the case. There is an obvious temptation to fault the Saudis and their laws. By Western standards, it is a repressive system with draconian punishments, especially in the treatment of women and citizens from third world nations. A type of social caste system, or social pecking order, exists, beginning with the royal family, filtering down to the many expatriates working as servants.

Indeed, there are vast differences in the way the Saudis and Islamic countries in general dispense justice as compared to the West. But we must understand that the kingdom of Saudi Arabia is still maturing politically and socially. It is only since 1932 that the kingdom developed any formalized government, with a constitution created in 1992 (Appendix B).

As history reminds us, civilization and social progress often coincide with economic development. However, some nations developed more slowly than others. With the introduction of oil in recent years, Saudi Arabia entered the fast track of development, becoming a serious player in the world economy, capturing the interest of oil-thirsty Western nations and assorted global opportunists seeking to cash in on the desert riches. In short, economic development outpaced political and social progress, at least from a Western perspective. While the Saudi Kingdom is often accused of human rights violations and unprogressive social policies, we must not forget that it took years after the United States created a constitution to eliminate slavery, desegregate schools, the military, and grant women the right to vote. And today, one can still find social division based on race or economic standing.

To embark on a campaign of condemning their culture and their human rights record only solicits counter-criticism of Western society and culture, particularly the United States, where violence is widespread and many poor families are forced to live in marginal housing or vermin infested slums. Additionally, the United States has the distinct record of imprisoning more people than any other Western nation. And, one can argue that the number of people in prison often defines the social progress (or lack of) of a society.

Even some skeptical British folk raise questions about punishment and administrating justice in the West. In the following news article, a British citizen eloquently criticizes justice administration in the West, raising the question as to who are the real barbarians. Are the Americans or British in any position to criticize the Arabs for their brand of justice?

WHO ARE THE BARBARIANS

I am against primitive punishment. I am against it whether the victim is male or female, British or foreign, guilty or innocent, nurse, drug dealer or common thief... I am not referring to the unlikely execution and flogging of two British nurses in Saudi Arabia. I refer to a punishment which received less publicity. A British judge, Gabriel Hutton, ordered that a pregnant 17-year-old from Gloucester, in jail for shoplifting, should have her baby removed from her at birth so she could go back to jail to complete her sentence. She had pleaded guilty to stealing four shirts worth £60 from Marks & Spencer. I venture that most foreigners would use the word barbaric of this punishment. In Saudi Arabia, pregnant women are automatically reprieved for two years after giving birth. Most Britons are inured to the cruelty of a penal tradition still obsessed with retribution. Most would read about the 17-year-old, shrug and say she deserved it. The judge went out of his way to remark that being deprived of the baby was part of the punishment. This is a disproportionate response to stealing four shirts. It is the emotional equivalent of chopping off a hand. It is medieval... The protest at the Saudi sentences is vulnerable to hypocrisy on almost every score. I wonder if those now raising a hue and cry would do the same were the prisoner male bankers rather than female nurses. At this moment, a British businessman is facing electrocution on death row in Florida for a double murder 11 years ago that all seem to agree he did not commit. The Briton, Chris Maharaj, has the misfortune to be non-white, male and not a nurse. He appears to have been stitched up for a murder and tried by a judge later arrested for corruption, but had insufficient money to pursue his defense.

Britons view America differently from Saudi Arabia. The former's penchant for frying alive those who might (or might not) have committed murder is a minor blot on the transatlantic friendship, best not mentioned in polite company. Besides, American justice is America's business; moral outrage is an easy cloak for prejudice. American are good Christian people, so we should not complain when they behave like, say, Arabs. Britain has some of the most crowded and backward prisons in the developed world. Britain has emerged from the past decade with a policy on punishment scarcely more sophisticated than that of Third World countries it loves to pillory. There may be a beam in our Saudi brother's eye. In our own there is a mighty mote.

—Simon Jenkins, The Times, 9/27/97

In any society, those on the lower end of the food chain haven't funds to retain high priced lawyers. But if you have the money you can hire a team of lawyers and experts that would terrify a pack of rabid jackals. Justice may be blind, but in some respects can be bought, negotiated, or manipulated to the satisfaction of the client. And to an extent, as we will see, this is what happened in the Gilford case.

2

CULTURAL JUSTICE

"To each among you, we have prescribed a law and a clear way."
—**Koran 5:48**

It is inappropriate to write of the Gilford case, or for that matter delve into a discussion of Saudi justice, without explaining the culture of Kingdom; to understand any culture requires an appreciation of its people, religion, laws, and of course the justice process. In many ways, culture drives law and justice, particularly in nations where religion dominates life and politics. And what better way to begin than with a discussion of Islam, the soul of Saudi culture.

Religion and Law

Islam is one of the dominant world religions. Islamic nations dot the globe from Africa, throughout the Middle East, Europe, and Asia. There are 35 nations with population over 50% Muslim, and another 21 nations that have a significant number of areas occupied with Muslims. Overall, the Muslim population is estimated at over 1.2 billion, translating to over 20% of the world's population. Significant Muslim populations reside in many Western nations as well. In London, the city is home to over one million Muslim; and it is estimated by the year 2000, one out of every four persons on the planet will be a Muslim. Nineteen nations have included Islamic guidelines in their respective constitutions. There is no doubt; the Muslim religion is a global one, rapidly expanding both economically, politically and socially.

Islam is an Arabic word denoting submission, surrender and

obedience. It literally means no religion other than Islam may be practiced within its borders. As a religion, Islam stands for complete submission and obedience to Allah. The second and alternate literal meaning of the word "Islam" is "peace." Common ground exists between the major Western religions and Islam. Muslims, as with Christians and Jews, are considered "children of the book," believing in one God.

As with some Christians and Jews, not all Muslims or Islamic nations follow religious teachings to the same extent. The United Arab Emirates, Egypt, and Kuwait are more liberal in their customs and tolerance to Western influences. Muslim nations such as Saudi Arabia, Iran, and Afghanistan are more restrictive and conservative. However, Saudi Arabia, while considered a religiously conservative nation, is more progressive and open to Western nations than belligerent Iraq, Iran, and Libya. Saudi Arabia occupies a special if not precarious position in the Arab world due to politics and religion. Not only is Saudi Arabia the major oil producer in the world, but it also holds an extraordinary place in Islam because the country is the birthplace and heartland of Islamic religion.

The followers of Islam in Saudi Arabia, known as Muslims, are split into two factions. The dominant group, about 85 percent of the population, is made up of Sunnah Muslims. The remaining 15 percent are referred to as Shiite Muslims. The few Shiite Muslims reside in the eastern portion of the country but are more predominant in other Islamic nations such as Iran. We often hear about disputes between the two sects. While both sects believe in one God and the Prophet Mohammed, they disagree on matters concerning politics and religious philosophy. The differences are analogous to right wing Christian fundamentalists clashing with more liberal religions in Western society, or disagreements between orthodox and mainstream religions. Some Western religions, in other words, differ on religious philosophy, the teachings of Jesus and so forth. Similarly, there is a long history of strained relations between the two Islamic sects.

Religious development in any society comes after some form of society or government (however barbaric or crude) has been established. We often look toward higher authorities to make sense out of messes made by mankind, and the pre-Islamic period of history for Arabs was a miserable state. Before the birth of the prophet Mohammed, many Arabs lived a nomadic, warlike existence, fighting over trivial matters.

The nomadic, desert culture people known as Bedouins was a culture based on ranching and farming, encouraging values of clan solidarity, and isolation from the rest of world. There was no formal government, usury was common, and all transactions were based on tradition. Social justice was unheard of and slavery part of the social fabric. We will explore more on the social and political development of the Kingdom later.

As to religious teachings, the Koran, the primary document of the Islamic faith, provided the believer spiritual and intellectual nourishment. Its major themes include the oneness of God, the purpose of human existence, faith and God-consciousness, and the Hereafter and its significance. The Koran places heavy emphasis upon reason and understanding. In short, it is believed that a true believer of the Koran is nurtured in the heart, the soul, and the mind just as many Christians experience when reading the Bible, attending a religious revival, or for some secular humanists reading philosophy or poetry?

Like many religions, there are a number of practices defining Islam's ideology, such as prayer. Five times a day shops close and Muslim men go the nearest mosque for prayers, while non-Muslims and women wait outside the shops for the duration of a prayer, which can last from 30 to 45 minutes. Not everyone is required to pray, but most businesses cease operating during prayer.

Like the celebration of Christmas for Christians or Hanukah for Jews, Ramadan is the holiest time in the Islamic year. Travel is difficult, and business is rarely conducted during the nearly-month-long observance of prayer and fasting during daylight hours.

In Saudi Arabia, it is foolhardy to display or wear a symbol of any other religion while in public, or condemn the Islamic religion in any way. Street corner and bicycle Evangelists, commonly found in Western nations, are not tolerated. Those who attempt to preach or practice missionary work of another faith are briskly hustled off to jail. So to are practices that suggest black magic or paganism. Such New Age beliefs such as astrology, tarot reading and other similar forms of practice are considered witchcraft and therefore illegal. As in any society, there are those who faithfully follow religious teachings and those who ignore religion. While there are obvious public restrictions, one may find in some private homes' satellite TV, computers and other western pleasures. Homes are considered sanctuaries, where life for some Saudis is far less restrictive. Outside of the home, major cities boast modern shopping malls, elegant hotels, resorts and restaurants.

Western cultural influences are not welcomed by all. The royal family, for example, is often accused of cuddling up closely with Western countries. And the presence of Western influences irritates religious fundamentalists. They view such extravagance as "poison" to the Islamic culture, which is why the royal family must tread carefully in efforts to modernize a country that is the home of Islam. In other words, not all Saudis share in Western indulgences, and there is a fear too many outside influences will provoke discontent or subversive ideas in the population.

Therefore there is a separation of private and public societies, or a type of private and public culture.

In spite of the desert landscape's alluring beauty and modernized cities, travel into this country is strictly limited. Over five million expatriates, or foreign workers, generally live in compounds near major cities. As invited guests, expatriates are expected to follow Islamic law and custom when in public. Visitors are warned that social practices and freedoms taken for granted in Western countries are not tolerated in Saudi Arabia. Exceptions are granted for approved business ventures and Saudi-sponsored visits. With eighteen million residents, Saudi Arabia is not accessible to tourists. This is not to suggest that Saudis are isolationists, or loathe tourism; it is just that their country's infrastructure and social taboos are not designed for tourists' demands or Kodak moments, especially by pampered Westerners with condescending attitudes.

When in public, attire worn by most Westerner women, such as shorts and tight jeans, are not to be worn unless covered with an ankle length gown known as an abaya. In other words, visitors seeking Western style pleasures and comforts will be disappointed. Drinking alcohol in public is strictly forbidden, as is dating between expatriates and Saudi citizens (unless the expatriate becomes a Muslim). There are no dance clubs, movie theaters, sports bars, casinos, Wrestle-mania or pork chops (pork is a forbidden meat under Islam). As stated by one former expatriate, "Saudi Arabia is not a country where you go clubbing, or sing karaoke."

Sexual Division

As with most of Arab society, men dominate family and social life. Women are considered property of their fathers or husbands. As stated in the Koran, *"Men have authority over women because God has made one more superior to the other and because they spend their wealth to maintain them. (Women 4:26)."* Of course, this statement is not admired by all Saudi women, especially those who embrace a more independent notion of the women's role in modern Saudi society. Yet, many Muslim women firmly follow this edict, believe in it, and should not be condemned, particularly by western feminists.

Under Islam, a man may have up to four wives, if he can afford them and has the energy. And indeed, a number of the Saudi aristocracy have more than one wife. While Western men may find this appealing, each wife must be provided for the same. No slacking or favoritism is allowed. Of course, divorce for men is much easier, with the man uttering the words "I divorce you." According to Islamic tradition, if a man intends to divorce his wife, "he should make sure that she is not in her menstruation period and that the two of them have not had sexual intercourse during her current period of cleanliness from menstruation." Women can also seek divorce if she can show a pattern of abuse or unfair treatment, and do have property rights.

The role of the modern Saudi woman is changing, albeit slowly. The latest independent statistics show the employment of women nearly doubled between 1986 and 1991 to 83,000, but 72,000 of these were foreigners. Nonetheless, the several thousand Saudi women that work do so in a wide range of fields, including medicine, education and business. Increasing numbers run their own companies and buy shares in Saudi firms. Women are finding increasing employment opportunities in the hospitality (hotel and resort) industry as well. Whenever possible, however, women are separated from men in such work environments. And women must wear the customary abaya and veils.

Saudi women (except those beyond their childbearing years) are subject to arrest for prostitution if found socializing in public with a man who is not a relative. According to the prophet Mohammed, *"Every eye is an adulterer; and every woman perfumeth herself, and goeth to an assembly where men are, wishing to show herself to them, with a look of lasciviousness, is an adulteress."* As explained later, adultery is one of the most serious offenses a Muslim can commit, resulting in serious punishment if proven.

When in public, Muslim women, as well as Western women are expected to cover their heads in public. Foreigners are given some leeway in the matter of dress, but they are expected to follow local customs, particularly in public places such as restaurants and malls. As a general rule, foreign men wear long trousers and shirts that cover the upper torso. Foreign women should wear loose fitting skirts with hemlines well below the knee. Sleeves should be at least elbow length and the neckline modest.

The best fashion advice is to "conceal rather than reveal." Teenagers are also required to dress modestly in public places. Jeans should not be tight fitting and low necks and tank tops are not recommended. Shorts and bathing suits should not be worn in public. Whatever their job or social status, Saudi men wear the traditional dress called a thobe. Wearing the thobe expresses equality and is also perfectly suited to the hot Saudi climate. During warm and hot weather, Saudi men and boys wear white thobes. During the cool weather, wool thobes in dark colors are not uncommon. At special times, men often wear a bisht or mishlah over the thobe. These are long white, brown or black cloaks trimmed in gold.

Public display of sexual affection, like kissing, holding hands and hugging is not tolerated. This is not to suggest that the Saudis are prudish or boorish however. Dancing, for example, should not aim at arousing unacceptable emotions or make of the woman's body the object of exciting desires. Many communities participate in folk dancing and it is acceptable, as the dancers are respectably dressed and the dance involves elaborate but proper movements.

Video stores and coffee shops are prominent in the major cities. However, magazines and videos deemed appropriate in the West are confiscated if they show men and women in revealing dress or socializing together. Censorship of books, magazines, film, etc. exists although some black-marketing does occur. Videos depicting expressions of sexual desire, including kissing, are censored. Advertising products using sex as the medium is not permitted. Visitors will not find product advertisements depicting scantily clad erotic maidens on billboards.

Under no circumstances are women permitted to drive automobiles, motorcycles, or even bicycles in public. In using public transportation, women must enter city buses by separate rear entrances and sit in specially designated sections. However, the driving ban on women may be changed.

In the changing economy of the Kingdom, it is becoming increasingly difficult to fund chauffeurs. In recent years, the Saudi oil economy has experienced a downward trend, forcing a reduction of service workers such as drivers for the women. Some Saudi men are annoyed by the driving restriction, because they must alter their schedules to drive their wives to various appointments.

However, despite their dependence on men, Saudi women are not passive or weak-willed, and have exhibited their defiance to Islamic rule. One example occurred in 1990 when fifty Saudi women defied the driving ban and motored through the capital city of Riyadh. But cheers gave way to quiet grumbling when the women were briefly detained and reports spread that several lost their jobs. In 1998, a Saudi news item offered hope that women may soon be able to drive legally in the Kingdom. A handbook on Saudi Arabia published by the Ministry of Information states, *"The stereotype of Muslim women as uneducated, barefooted, creatures with no rights and no opportunities is a caricature born of ignorance or malevolence."*

Across multiple settings and environments, sexual segregation clearly permeates the social fabric. One Saudi woman said, *"Universities are separated according to sex. Girls get to watch male teachers on television screens live and they can call in questions."* Most banks have special women's branches with all-female staff and customers. Restaurants are either for men only or offer an additional 'family section.' A common sign at Riyadh restaurants reads: "No Single Women" even in family sections. Women are not admitted to a hospital for medical treatment without the consent of a male relative, and women may not undertake domestic and foreign travel alone unless they have approval from a male relative, such as a husband, brother, or father. Why such strict segregation and chauvinism? The idea behind sexual restrictions is to limit actions and opportunities deemed sexually attractive to men. While these prohibitions undoubtedly would raise havoc with Western women, any protests would lead to deaf ears and any disobedience would possibly lead to a prompt invitation to leave the country.

Western Compounds

In spite of the conditions present in the dominant Muslim culture, the residential compounds for non-Saudi workers and families allow for discreet pleasures, offering sanctuaries of Western freedom. Most Westerners working in the Kingdom live in compounds where dress codes and other cultural formalities are relaxed. These self-contained communities are like a desert oasis, containing modern conveniences such as swimming pools, spas, cafeterias, entertainment, and a host of other recreational opportunities designed to make living easier for expatriates. Yes, one may even find bikini-clad Westerners lounging poolside, sipping a cocktail. According to expatriates who have lived in some of these compounds, prostitution occurs among some of the third world expatriates to "help meet expenses." This is not to say that morality crimes are rampant in all compounds, but it was alleged by a number of expatriates that such offenses occurred. The compounds are a welcome escape for expatriates trapped in a society bound by strict religious taboos. Once a Westerner ventures beyond the compound walls, respect for the culture is expected. Other than shopping, entertainment for Westerners is in the form of camping trips to the picturesque deserts, which make up nearly 90 percent of the landscape. Many expatriates who feel the urge to experience Western pleasures simply go on holiday, or travel to nearby United Arab Emirates. There they find more Western luxuries and relaxed religious customs.

Government and Law

As to law and government, the Kingdom is a sovereign Arab Islamic State, divided into 14 districts, each ruled by a Royal Prince. The government derives power from the Holy Koran and the Prophet's tradition. The King and his council of ministers, without the trappings of political parties or legislature, rule the country. Simply put, there are no election campaigns, petty politicking, or government lobbying prominent in Western nations. Nepotism and royal family connections replace elections. Even more so than in Western countries, in seeking a job it helps to know the right people.

Legal reform sprouted in 1992, resulting in the creation of a constitution. Contained in the document are eight chapters with 83 articles (Appendix B). The constitution, which is a simply a reflection of the Koran and Sunnah doctrine, was produced to clarify contemporary powers and duties of the government. In article five, chapter 2, for example, the system of government is explained as follows:

a) The system of government in the Kingdom of Saudi Arabia is that of a monarchy.

(b) Rule passes to the sons of the founding King, Abd al-Aziz Bin Abd al-Rahman al-Faysal Al Sa'ud, and to their children's children. The most upright among them is to receive allegiance in accordance with the principles of the Holy Koran and the Tradition of the Venerable Prophet.

(c) The King chooses the Heir Apparent and relieves him of his duties by Royal order.

(d) The Heir Apparent is to devote his time to his duties as an Heir Apparent and to whatever missions the King entrusts him with.

(e) The Heir Apparent takes over the powers of the King on the latter's death until the act of allegiance has been carried out.

In England by comparison, the royal family is primarily ceremonial, with important state decisions made by the Prime Minister and Parliament. In Saudi Arabia, the King is the chief executive of the country, who, along with his council of ministers, makes all state decisions. Articles 60—64 of the Saudi constitution (Appendix A) state clearly who is in political charge of the kingdom.

The origins of the modern kingdom of Saudi Arabia lie in the mid-18th century religious movement called *Wahhabism,* founded by Muhammad ibn Abd al-Wahhab. Prior to that time the nation was composed of various tribal groups. His movement was supported by Muhammad ibn Saud, a chieftain of a tribe, who helped spread *Wahhabi* doctrines and to reduce the rest of Arabia to the rule of the Al Saud family. The Wahhabis favor strict religious guidelines, and are credited with preserving the traditional values of the Islam in the Kingdom. One might view the Wahhabis as a conservative group favoring adherence to strict religious values, much like so called Southern Baptists in the United States, or various orthodox religious groups in other countries.

In 1927 Ibn Saud was recognized as king and sultan. Five years later, Ibn Saud changed the name of his kingdom to Saudi Arabia. It was immediately internationally recognized as an independent country. In 1933, the country finally emerged from the tribal factions that dominated the Kingdom for years. The Kingdom of Saudi Arabia was born, and in 1936 a treaty was signed with Yemen marking the southern borders of the Kingdom. Thus modern history of Saudi Arabia generally begins in the early 1930s. After a succession of royal family rulers, Fahd bin Abdul Aziz took control in 1982 and continues to rule the vast desert nation today. King Fahd is viewed as a reformer, streamlining the government and introducing new laws, but he also recognizes his principal duty as leader of a conservative Islamic state.

Continuing development within the country and the infrastructure marks King Fahd's reign. New highways were constructed, foreign industry was brought in, and trade relations with Western nations increased. Saudi Arabia is the largest oil producing country in the world, accounting for a quarter of the world's oil reserves. Over the years, however, the Kingdom has undergone criticism for its stance on human rights, and especially chastised by the Western press in regard to the nurses' dilemma. For the record, the Saudi government disagrees with internationally accepted definitions of human rights and views its interpretation of Islamic law as its sole source of guidance. An attack on their justice system or government is an attack on their religion, the very foundation of their culture and law.

The Sharia penetrates Saudi life, including business and social relations. The law regulates personal hygiene, diet, sexual conduct, and elements of child rearing. It prescribes specific rules for prayers, fasting, giving to the poor, and many other religious matters. Simply stated, the law deals with the ideology, faith, behavior, manners, and practical every day concerns.

Doing business with Saudis requires patience, something I learned quickly. The fast paced, often-impulsive negotiations of Western businessmen are not effective in the Kingdom. And the justice system is no exception. About the only fast-paced comparisons with the West are driving behaviors, with automobile accidents a serious problem in the Kingdom.

There is no division between church and state in Saudi Arabia as found in Western societies. Religion and law are intertwined. In fact, religion defines law. The Government does not permit the establishment of political parties and suppresses opposition views, with the Government restricting freedom of speech, the press, assembly, association, and religion.

In every society there is a source of law. In Great Britain and the United States, laws are based on common law or grounded on past cases, known as precedent. In Saudi Arabia, several sources translate the Sharia, or law of Islam. The two primary sources are the Koran and Sunnah. *The Koran* (sometimes spelled Quran) or Islamic scripture, contains the word of God as revealed to the prophet Mohammed. It is the primary document of Islam, legal or otherwise, and is considered the *"guide for life in this world and the hereafter."* It contains about 500 verses with instructions that could be taken as moral or legal injunctions and is somewhat like the Judeo-Christian Bible in terms of advice or moral guidance, but sometimes open to interpretation depending upon your belief.

The Sunnah is the collected words and acts of the prophet Mohammed as relayed to his companions. From the Islamic standpoint, Sunnah refers to anything narrated or related about the prophet Mohammad, authentically traced to him regarding his speech, actions, traits, and silent approvals. The following four principles establish the basis of the law. (1) Actions will be judged according to intentions. (2) The proof of a Muslim's sincerity is that he pays no heed to that which is not his business. (3) No man is a true believer unless he desires for his brother that which he desires for himself. (4) That which is lawful is clear, and that which is unlawful likewise, but there are certain doubtful things between the two from which it is well to abstain.

An example of one of Mohammad's sayings, and a reflection of the above principles, is offered below: *"Actions are judged by their intentions; everyone will be rewarded according to his/her intention. So whoever migrates for the sake of Allah and His Prophet then his migration will be noted as a migration for the sake of Allah and His Prophet. Conversely, one who migrates only to obtain something worldly or to marry a woman, then his migration will be worth what he had intended."*

The above passage makes a great deal of moral sense if you think about it. One who helps another for the pure sake of helping is acting with good intention. On the other hand, one who helps for the purpose of future reward is acting immorally--marrying for money, for example, is not love. It is an action with a wrong intention.

The age of modernization and change in Saudi Arabia has forced the Sharia to consider other sources beyond the teachings of the Koran and sayings of the prophet Mohammed. Such sources include the Ijma, the Qiyas, and royal decrees.

The Muslim religion uses the term Ulama as a label for its religious scholars or teachers. These Ulamas are consulted on many matters both personal and political. When the Ulamas reach a consensus on an issue, it is interpreted as Ijma, or a type of binding arbitration. You will not find the concepts and ideas of the Ijma in the Koran or the teachings of the Prophet (Sunnah). Islamic judges are able to examine the ijma for many possible solutions that can be applied in a modern technical society. Thus, Ijma is referred to as a third source of law.

The Qiyas are a fourth source of Sharia Law. The Qiyas are not explicitly found in the Koran, Sunnah, or given in the Ijma. The Qiyas are new cases or case law, which may have already been decided by a higher judge. The Sharia judge can use this legal precedent to decide new case law and its application to a specific problem.

The judge can use a broad legal construct to resolve a very specific issue. For example, a computer crime or theft of computer time is not found in the Koran or Sunnah. The act of theft as a generic term is prohibited, so the judge must rely on logic and reason to create new case law or Qiyas. This source of legal reasoning is one of the major foundations of Western law; to decide present cases based upon past decisions.

A final source of law is royal decrees by the king. Drug smuggling, for example, was made a capital offense in 1987 under a broad Sharia principle allowing the king to initiate laws to protect society from great dangers. Many legal obstacles found in Western justice systems simply do not exist in the kingdom. Game playing, showmanship, and other legal "rubbish" demonstrated in such famous American cases as the O.J. Simpson trial are absent in the Kingdom. In other words, the criminal justice process emphasis crime control which translates to less use of lawyers and due process. This is not to suggest that there are no rights, but that justice seems to move more quickly, with the outcomes more certain.

All persons in Saudi Arabia, including the king, royal family, and foreigners, are equal before the law and subject to Saudi law. In practice, however, members of the royal family and other important leaders have rarely been brought to public trial, and cases involving foreigners are often handled outside the court system, frequently resulting in prompt deportation. The administering of justice in Saudi Arabia follows many of the same processes found in Western societies. There is a hierarchy of law enforcement, courts and judges. Regarding law enforcement, police and border forces fall under the Ministry of Interior, a royal family member, who is responsible for internal security of the country. Each city has a police force, with a chain of command structure similar to police agencies in Western societies. Police officers receive training in traditional investigative techniques and enforcement procedures. A number of professional police experts from Western nations over the years have provided training to the Saudi police. Thus, the police are not totally "in the dark" when it comes to modern investigative practices.

The police, as we will learn, are responsible for investigating all crimes committed in Western compounds. In other words, everyone regardless of nationality is accountable under Saudi law and subject to arrest. In theory, the Saudi police are not authorized to employ Gestapo type tactics. The 1992 Saudi constitution expressly provides for rights and duties for arrest: *The state provides security for all its citizens and all residents within its territory and no one shall be arrested, imprisoned, or have their actions restricted except in cases specified by statutes (Chapter 5 article 36).*

Despite the law, there are examples of Saudi officers (much like their Western counterparts), who make arrests and detain persons without following explicit legal guidelines. Yet, abusive police practices are a problem in any society, including Saudi Arabia. If abuse occurs in the more progressive Western societies, then why would we not expect it in any other system? The London Metropolitan Police have been heavily criticized for racism, and there has been an ongoing investigation into corruption in the force. In a British news article reported on September 16, 1998, police officers in London were under criticism for corruption and racism from within their ranks. In 1997, the Metropolitan Police Commissioner, Sir Paul Condon, instituted undercover "integrity tests" as part of the anti-corruption strategy. Police departments in the United States also has its share of rogue and corrupt police officials. What is surprising about these acts of abuse is that the cities employing these officers have some of the highest recruitment and training standards in the world of policing.

In Western societies, there are recourses for unlawful arrest and abuse, known as law suits. Civil or constitutional rights investigations by federal authorities, such as the Federal Bureau of Investigation, may also be initiated against local police. Criminal charges may be filed as well. In Saudi Arabia there are few safeguards against abuse. One major reason is that Saudi Arabia has no free press scrutinizing the actions of public officials, as found in Western societies. Additionally, lawsuits are rare and police checks and balances are not as advanced.

Although the Saudi police must generally demonstrate reasonable cause and obtain permission from the provincial governor before searching a private home, warrants are not usually required. In accordance with a regulation issued by the Ministry of Interior in 1983, police may detain suspects for no longer than three days before charging them; however, serious exceptions have been reported.

The regulation provides for bail for less serious crimes, and detainees are sometimes released on the recognizance of a patron or sponsoring employer without the payment of bail. Prisoners not released on bail are detained an average of one to two months before going to trial.

In Western nations such as the United States, a person arrested for a crime must officially be charged within 48 or 72 hours (depending upon the state) or released. Bail release is available in most cases unless the offense is serious such as murder, or the offender is considered a risk or untrustworthy.

In the Kingdom, there is no established procedure providing detainees the right to inform their family of arrest. In the case of foreigners, Saudi authorities usually confirm the arrest to their country's diplomats only when asked. In general, foreign diplomats learn about such arrests through informal channels, such as co-workers or family.

Allegations by Amnesty International cite evidence that in capital cases, foreigners in the past have been tried and executed without notification of their arrest or even given the right to meet with their government's representatives. Expatriates from Third World nations (Pakistan, Philippines, etc.) are generally not accorded the same degree of fairness or justice as Western expatriates. Even, In Western compounds, expatriates from Third World nations are housed in different buildings. Again, social status and government interests often supersede justice, a truism in any society, like it or not!

Aside from the regular law enforcement agencies, there is the Mutawwa'in, or religious police. This branch is a component of the Committee to Prevent Vice and Promote Virtue, a semiautonomous agency that encourages adherence to Islamic values by monitoring public behavior. Although they often take their role too seriously, reports of harassment, intimidation, and detention of those deemed to be violating the moral code declined in 1995 and 1996.

Anyone who has spent time in the Kingdom has witnessed their work. The Mutawwa'in are a type of security force, assisting the regular police in controlling every aspect of Saudi life. The primary function of the Mutawwa'in is to see that all shops are closed during prayer times, and to watch for signs of other religions being practiced. Although the Mutawwa'in are not regular police, they have the authority to detain people for behavior violations and often deliver violators to the regular Saudi police.

In many areas of Saudi Arabia, particularly Riyadh and the central part of the Kingdom, Mutawwa'in pressure women to wear the full-length black abaya and to cover their heads. Most women in these areas wear the abaya and carry a headscarf to avoid harassment. Women who appear to be of Arab or Asian origin, especially those presumed to be Muslims, face a greater risk of scrutiny, but Western women are constantly reminded to conform to the customs.

Unfortunately, a number of expatriates have found themselves in Saudi custody for various behavior violations. However, in recent years, due to open confrontations and complaints, the government has exerted tighter control over the *Mutawwa'in,* pressuring them to follow established procedures and to offer instruction to the public in a polite manner. Thus, the Mutawwa'in's enforcement role has diminished in recent years due to reduced government funding. There is also the fear that if the moral police are not restrained, the people will resist causing unnecessary problems for the royal family.

The Saudi monarchy is intolerant of persons who denounce the government. Detainees arrested by the General Directorate of Investigation (GDI), which is the Ministry of Interior's security service, are commonly held incommunicado in special prisons during the initial phase of an investigation, which may last weeks or months. Detainees are only allowed limited contact with their families or lawyers. Civil disobedience is not tolerated, authorities will detain without charge people who publicly criticize the government, or charge them with attempting to destabilize the Government. As of this writing, Saudi authorities continued to detain Salman Al-Awdah and Safar Al-Hawali, Muslim clerics who were arrested in September 1994 for publicly criticizing the government. Their detention sparked protest demonstrations resulting in the arrest of 157 persons for antigovernment activities.

At the end of 1994, 27 of these persons remained in detention pending investigation, and the government did not announce the release of any of those detainees in the succeeding two years. The thousands of prisoners and detainees released under the annual Ramadan amnesty included no political dissidents.

One certain way of gaining police attention and ultimate wrath of the Saudi government is to perform missionary work in the Kingdom. Promoting religions other than Islam is a serious crime, ranked with civil disobedience, and potentially punishable by death. In June 1998, several Christians were arrested in Riyadh for distributing Christian literature. Reports of torture and abuse of the arrestees surfaced. In addition, the homes of the arrestees were searched and their computer databases examined. A Filipino pastor was arrested, tortured and sentenced to death in 1992, but was deported to the Philippines instead.

One expatriate Christian previously detained by Saudi authorities described interrogation by the religious police.

"First they beat you," the source said. *"Then in the midst of the pain they heap verbal abuse and mental torture on you. Then they beat you again while they question you. If they don't believe you are answering truthfully, they will torture you more."* (Quotes from Evangelical Press News Service, 1998)

In the absence of a confession, witnesses must be found for some offenses. Due to the high standard of evidence needed, the pressure to get one to confess may go beyond reason and fairness, which is an issue in the Gilford case.

Courts and Trials

General trials in Saudi Arabia are presided over by judges termed Qadis. Judges are legal scholars appointed to hear complaints and cross-examine plaintiffs, defendants, and any witnesses. Unlike some Western nations, Saudi judges actively participate in the trial process, asking questions, evaluating evidence, and making sure correct procedures are followed. In serious cases, Saudi judges often anguish over their decisions, fearful they may be judged in the next life, as they have judged in this life. An Islamic saying states: *"For every three judges, two will go to the Fire and only one to Paradise."* Trials are often referred to as arbitrations, with an attempt to reach a compromise by the opposing parties. Some suggest trials are a form of legal bartering between the various parties, like deciding the price of a melon in the marketplace.

Judges in Saudi Arabia belong to the Hanbalis School of Islamic law, allowing judges wide discretion in deciding cases. Imam Hanbali, its founder, detested political power, frequently upsetting rulers of his time and refusing to change even when he was tortured. The Saudi judiciary idealizes Hanbali and many judges openly try to emulate him. While Judges base their interpretations of the law, on the crime and the offender, they may not undermine or supersede the Koran or Sunnah.

Courts apply rules of the Islamic Sharia in the cases that are brought before them, in accordance with what is indicated in the Koran and the Sunnah, and statutes decreed by the Ruler that do not undermine the Koran or the Sunnah. They follow diligently the Koranic verses that declare:

O ye who believe, stand out firmly for justice, as witness of God, even as against yourselves, or your parents, or your kin. follow not the lust of your heart lest you swerve, and if you distort justice or decline to do justice, verily God is well acquainted with all that you do. (4:135).

The forum for trials is vastly different in the desert Kingdom. Generally, there are three levels of Sharia courts. The first level or so-called trial level is presided over by one or often three judges. Of the three, there is usually a senior more experienced judge who carries the most clout. Occasionally the judges may haggle over a legal point, delaying the proceedings. Missing from the courtroom are battles pitting a tough politically-oriented prosecutor against a tireless defense attorney out to plant reasonable doubt in the minds of the jury.

Trial by jury is unknown under the Sharia, and all trials are closed to the public. Plea-bargaining, a common method of diverting cases from trial in the United States, does not exist. Also absent are public defenders and court-appointed criminal defense attorneys. Lawyers have no court role in criminal matters because Saudi judges believe they will obscure the truth, a belief I have little argument with. Lawyers have a role in the Kingdom, but are more reserved for civil or business matters, both domestically and Internationally.

When a judgment is made (and this may take some time), no appeal can be made, but a dissatisfied party can object to the decision. If this occurs, the case will proceed to the court of Cassation, a type of review court, just to make sure that the judge has paid sufficient attention to the objection or facts. There is neither re-examination of the facts, re-trial, nor review of witness statements except in limited circumstances. It rarely occurs that this court could disagree with the earlier court, causing the case to be reviewed again. However, if the Cassation court agrees with the finding of the first court, and the case is serious (e.g. murder), the matter reverts to the high judicial council, the highest judicial authority in the Kingdom (equivalent to the House of Lords in England or the Supreme Court in the United States). If the Supreme Judicial Council overturns the judgment, the case will start again with a different court.

If the Supreme Council endorses the judgments of capital punishment reached by the two earlier courts, the matter is referred to the Royal Court for the King to give permission to proceed with the implementation of the ruling. Judicial experts in the Royal Court only issue such orders after intensive final review.

The King is the final appeal authority. This lengthy process, which usually takes between a year and two years depending on the details of the case, is designed to guarantee that no harsh sentence is passed lightly. It is possible the king may reduce a murder from intentional to unintentional if he feels the facts warrant. If the murder is found to be intentional, and the king does not intervene, the family of the deceased has a right to request the death penalty or demand blood money. This will be addressed in more detail in Chapter seven.

By comparison, in the United States, the Supreme Court is the final appellate authority, while in Great Britain the House of Lords is the highest judicial authority. While the Saudi judicial system is linked to religion, the American and British systems of justice are based on codified laws. Great Britain's law is based sources such as a Bill of Rights and law in the United States is based on the Constitution, court laws, and so forth.

We know that in Great Britain and the United States, offenders are presumed innocent until proven guilty. This requirement is also true in Saudi Arabia, under Islam, where the more serious the crime, the more evidence needed to convict. Either a voluntary confession of the accused or credible eyewitnesses are needed to establish evidence of a crime. As we will learn later, the confession is primary determination of guilt.

Since the Sharia relies heavily on witnesses, they must meet certain criteria. First, witnesses must be persons of sound moral character. Second, they must be mature; over the age of puberty. Third, witnesses must be sane both during the time of the offense and when offering testimony. Finally, witnesses must not have been convicted of a serious crime or engaged in deviant behavior.

As in other nations, witness credibility is also an integral part of the justice process. Witnesses who lack honesty are excluded from testifying or are impeached, meaning their testimony is without value. In Western societies, witnesses may be cross-examined by lawyers. In Saudi Arabia, judges determine witness credibility or their truthfulness. Lawyers play no role in examining witnesses.

Hanbali jurists rely more on their own direct cross-examination of the plaintiff and the accused than on written testimony. Judges insist that the accused speak openly and without duress. Even when the accused has already confessed, judges want to hear the confessions themselves, assuring that the confessions are free and voluntary.

In the Gilford case, the police wanted the nurses' confessions to be as accurate as possible, recognizing that the judges would want assurances that the confessions were free and voluntary. In theory, Sharia Judges follow the tradition of the Prophet: *"Set aside punishment where there is doubt."* Or, in short, they are looking for areas of doubt. However, by the time a defendant reaches the judge, he or she may be so worn out from police questioning that they are ready to confess just to end the ordeal.

Saudi court sessions usually last from five minutes to two hours. As previously noted, the accused are not defended by lawyers and are denied the opportunity to cross-examine witnesses, offer witnesses in their favor, or present any other evidence crucial to their defense. This means that the defense is limited to answering questions posed by the judge or judges.

In criminal cases, the defense attorney plays a passive role (with the exception of the Gilford case, as we will learn), concerned mainly with translation and interpreting law. If a defendant is found guilty and the right to compensation is decided on, the judge attempts to arrive at fair reparation acceptable to both parties.

Saudi courts are notorious for keeping offenders in limbo. Basically, little information is available because of the restricted role of defense lawyers, and absence of media coverage. The process in arriving at a punishment is painfully slow, but ultimately certain. While there is an appellate process, prisoners indicate they had no knowledge or idea of judicial "appeal" or judicial reviews; and prisoners, especially non-Western offenders, are rarely informed of their case progress. Detainees in cases involving the death sentence live under constant fear of being called out at any moment to be executed. This was the fear for the nurses. They never knew what the court decided. Most information came from outsiders or rumors from within the prison. For those unfortunate souls facing charges of death, the first sign of their ultimate fate is when they are taken from their cell to meet their executioner. One expatriate who had no knowledge of the progress of his case except that the charges carried the death penalty, wrote of the uncertainty:

"...each day that I'm here in prison, I'm always scared, especially Fridays because that's the day when they execute those who are on death row...I'm always scared, thinking I may be executed next...(one prisoner here) was beheaded on the first Friday of May."

In a letter to Amnesty International, the same prisoner reported being taken to see a judge after eleven months in detention, still having no clear idea about the progress of the case. Later, after almost five years in prison, the prisoner still unclear about the case wrote:

"... I'm still not quite sure as they haven't summoned me to court yet. I am still not able to speak with the judge and in a matter of months it will be five years that I have been here. My mind is tired from thinking all the time... I'm always taking sleeping pills to help me sleep... Even though I am taking sleeping pills, I can only sleep from 4:00 a.m. to 7:00 a.m."

Amnesty International reports a number of cases of abuse by the Saudi police and justice system. I cite one example because the case involves an expatriate who had been working in the Kingdom for several years. The case is referred to as the ordeal of Donato Lama, a Filipino national working in Saudi Arabia for 15 years. His unfortunate ordeal began on 11 October, 1995, in Riyadh, when five plain clothes policemen came to his home and told him that he was wanted for questioning about a murder case. Lama told them that he knew nothing about it, but they proceeded to search his house without a warrant, and found a photograph of him attending a Christian prayer meeting with others and a pamphlet about Islam. They then took him, without any arrest warrant, to the Police Station in Riyadh, where they held him incommunicado for two weeks.

Lama was interrogated repeatedly while shackled and handcuffed, and beaten to confess to being a Christian preacher. He admitted to being a Christian but denied the preaching charge. He was told that if he signed a statement written in Arabic, he would be released. In reality, the statement he thought was a "release clearance" was in fact a "confession" to being a Christian preacher. He was transferred to Malaz Prison and left waiting without explanation. His waiting came to an end over a year later on 26 November, 1996 when his jailers suddenly chained his legs, handcuffed him and took him to a court in Riyadh. His trial hearing lasted between 15 and 20 minutes, during which he stood shackled and handcuffed in front of the judge who questioned him about preaching Christianity.

On 16 December, 1996, he was returned to the court and sentenced to 18 months imprisonment and 70 lashes. The judge told him he could appeal if he did not accept the sentence. Aware that he had only about four more months left to serve (in view of the time he had already spent in detention), and that other prisoners who had opposed court verdicts had ended up serving longer sentences, he accepted the sentence even though he did not accept the guilty verdict. Lama served his prison term and the lashes were carried out in one single session, leaving him with bleeding and badly bruised back and legs.

Donato Lama told Amnesty International: *"I was examined by a doctor before the flogging who certified that I was fit to receive the lashes, but I had no medical examination after the lashing."*

Like the McLauchlan and Parry ordeal a little over a year later, the Lama case involved an alleged tricked confession, denial of due process, and other assorted abuses. Amnesty International cites dozens of examples of cases where both Saudi citizens and expatriates have been detained and harassed for flimsy reasons. Remember, these are allegations based on anecdotal information and on interviews with the victims, themselves. And, up until the nurses' case, there was no evidence of substantive legal representation for any defendant. (see: Amnesty International's Urgent Action: Execution/ Flogging/ Legal concern, 15 August, 1995, AI Index: MDE 23/05/95).

In serious cases, the judge may suggest appropriate punishment, but he (there are no women judges in Saudi Arabia yet) does not pass sentence. After he has made his determination, the record of trial is sent to the provincial governor who, with the advice of the local ulama or religious scholar, pronounces sentence. Cases involving crimes punishable by death or amputation are heard by panels of three judges, a type of appellate review in the Kingdom.

The King reportedly reviews all cases (although it is not clear how aggressively) where execution or amputation is the punishment. Yet, this may be a perfunctory process in some cases. However, in a murder conviction, as with Deborah Parry in the Yvonne Gilford murder case, when the victim's family demands death (assuming no blood money is negotiated or the murder is reduced to a non-intentional killing by the king which has on occasion been done), the sentence of death must be carried out; neither the courts nor the King can intervene if the murder is truly intentional or carried out with specific intent to kill. In other words, the Sharia does not recognize manslaughter killings, which are killings without criminal intent, but resulting from recklessness or negligence of the accused.

Like the gowns and veils concealing a woman's figure, secrecy shrouds the entire justice process. When a guilty verdict is returned and a sentence passed, defendants are asked by the judge if they accept the sentence. For those who accept the sentence, punishment is imposed. When a sentence is challenged and in all cases of capital punishment and amputation, the case is referred to the higher courts for "appeal" or judicial review.

In an Australian interview, Muslim scholar Abdullah Saeed, Head of Islamic studies at Melbourne University, stated *"If there is any kind of doubt, the judge should avoid implementing the punishment, even though the judge might believe that the person is guilty."* (interview July 10, 1997).

Crime and Punishment

A major purpose of law and punishment in any society is to control crime and violence because, unfortunately, not everyone follows moral decrees of society. Despite an abundance of laws, street violence and lawlessness in Western society is rampant. Yet the Kingdom is relatively immune from violence normally associated with Western nations. You will not find roving street gangs, open prostitution, or street violence common in so-called advanced democratic societies. This does not mean that violence is absent in the Kingdom. There are incidences of murder, robbery, and rape. Occasionally, reports surface of servants attacking their employers or vice versa. In 1999, news reports from the Kingdom described attempted school shootings by disgruntled students. It seems the pattern of school violence prominent in the United States that year somehow found its way to the Kingdom, where gun control is very strict and punishment severe for those who intentionally harm another.

It is not known how much crime actually occurs or is reported, especially among the Bedouin class residing in smaller towns and outlying desert communities. But the frequency of these crimes is considerably less than in Western societies, and temptations or opportunities to commit such offenses are fewer. For example, there are no liquor stores, strip clubs, or gambling casinos punctuating the desert landscape. The toxic culture found in the west is absent in the Kingdom.

A British citizen employed in Saudi Arabia writes of the difference between safety in England and Saudi Arabia in his letter to the London Daily Telegraph in 1997:

"Why was it that, within six months of returning to a 'civilized' country, I was threatened at a local bus stop by a gang of youths? Why is it that, as a law abiding citizen, I would fear for my life walking around the back streets of London? Why was it that, when I lived in an 'uncivilized' country for six years, there was not one single occasion when I was remotely threatened by anyone? Why was I able to walk around the back streets of Riyadh without a worry in the world?"

—Graham Tomlin, Northwich, Cheshire,
The Daily Telegraph, 9/25/97

Of the few violent crimes, most are isolated cases directed toward foreigners, particularly government officials and military personnel, as in the case of the 1996 bombing in Dhahran. The reason for the violence is attributed to the feelings by some more militant Saudis that western influences, particularly the military, is an intrusion upon their society. As in Western societies, persons acquainted or known to each other cause most of the problems resulting from business disputes (illegal or otherwise) or a personal relationship gone sour.

Why the low reported crime rates? Perhaps reasons are the relatively homogeneous state of the population, the religion, emphasis on family unity, social restrictions, or severity of the sanctions imposed for criminal violations. Severe punishments, such as beheading and amputation, are carried out in public, adding particular meaning to the concept of teaching by example. But, despite these gruesome public spectacles, violent crimes do occur occasionally.

With the influx of expatriates in the early 1970s, incidents of theft, murder and violent crimes increased, but such crimes remain relatively rare, confined to certain areas and persons acquainted with each other. There are few official crime statistics released in Saudi Arabia, but one comparative study from the 1980s suggests that the level of crime on a per-capita basis is about 1/30th of Ohio, a typical U.S. state. Anecdotal evidence indicates a crime rate that, by Western standards, is infinitesimal.

Supporting data released by the Arab organization for social defense, compared murder, property crimes, and sexual offenses of seven Arab nations (Saudi Arabia, Syria, Sudan, Egypt, Iraq, Lebanon, and Kuwait). In the 10-year study from 1970 through 1979, Saudi Arabia had the lowest number of reported crimes and rates of any Arab nation.

In the case of murder, for example, Saudi Arabia averaged 53 murders, or a rate of less than one per 100,000 people, the lowest of all Arab nations. By comparison, Lebanon had the highest murder rate (12.5 per 100,000 people), averaging 439 over the 10-year period. Saudi Arabia had the lowest number and rate of property and sex crimes as well.

The United States Department of State provides information on all nations relative to crime, security, travel advisories, and other information. Saudi Arabia is described as a relatively safe country, with few incidents of violent crime. However, the State Department warns of the potential of attacks on Westerners; and penalties for the import, manufacture, possession, and consumption of alcohol or illegal drugs are severe. Convicted offenders can expect jail sentences, fines, public flogging, and/or deportation, with the penalty for drug trafficking as death. No Westerner has been executed in Saudi Arabia to date, although a number have been detained in Saudi prisons, some for several years.

In Western societies, crime is divided into categories of seriousness, as defined by the harm to society and punishment imposed. Serious crimes are treason, which is a crime against the government and includes the acts of spying and foreign espionage. A conviction of intentional or premeditated murder may result in life imprisonment or death. Retribution is practiced in the kingdom; Yet, the Koran did not introduce the principle of retribution, but merely reaffirmed what is written in the Old Testament.

There are three primary divisions of crime in the Kingdom. The first is termed Huddud crimes, or moral crimes specifically defined as with set punishment provided by the Koran or *Sunnah*. In Huddud offenses, the rules of evidence are more rigorous because these crimes are viewed as extremely serious. In adultery and slander accusations, for example, four credible male witnesses are needed to convict the accused. At any time, a witness can retract his statement without fear of punishment.

The seven Huddud crimes include the following:

1. Adultery, for which punishment is stoning.

2. Illegal fornication or pre marital sexual conduct resulting in punishment of 100 lashes.

3. False accusation of adultery, for which punishment is 80 lashes.

4. Apostasy (renouncing Islam) brings death.

5. Drinking alcohol, 80 lashes.

6. Theft, for which punishment can be amputation of the right hand.

7. Highway robbery, for which the punishment is the amputation of feet or, if murder was involved, death by sword or crucifixion.

Since these crimes are violations of the Koran or moral violations, they are viewed as extremely serious. The evidence requires a voluntary confession from the accused, or testimony from two male witnesses (other than adultery, which requires four). If the confession is withdrawn and there is no other evidence, the judge cannot impose punishment under the Huddud category. In these crimes, a confession without witnesses or other evidence is not enough to convict. Likewise, judges must be 100 percent convinced that the confession was voluntary.

In spite of the seriousness of these crimes, the punishments are not always carried out, because of the required proof. To be punished for adultery, the Koran requires four adult male witnesses to the offense, a difficult standard of evidence to meet. Execution for adultery is public stoning to death for the woman and public beheading for the man, although the tough evidence standard assures the sentence is rarely administered in Saudi Arabia.

Regarding theft, the amputation of a hand or foot usually is not done unless the accused is a repeat offender, the theft involves a breaking or entering, or involves serious injury as in the case of strong-armed robbery. A petty thief who steals out of necessity (hunger) will not necessarily lose a limb over the matter. No one, for example, would lose his hand for embezzlement, forgery, stealing public money, or helping himself to items not properly protected.

We often hear of theft offenders in Saudi Arabia getting their hands chopped off. Yet this information is a bit exaggerated; true, theft is one of the serious Hadd offenses (Hadd is the singular of Huddud), punishable by amputation. But there is a procedure that must be followed.

To constitute a prima facie case of theft (prima facie means evidence which stands on its face as valid unless other evidence is offered to contradict it) the accused must have reached the age of puberty. Like Western law, children are excused of criminal liability if they are too young to know what is right or wrong (generally under the age of 16 years).

However, a juvenile may be tried as an adult if the crime is particularly heinous and the offender was of sound mind. So how does a thief lose a limb? The chances of losing a hand increases dramatically if the accused is convicted of a serious theft offense, such as armed robbery, and there are at least two credible witnesses. Under Saudi law, the accused must have committed the crime through deceit, such as entering a place without consent and committing a theft, as in unlawful entry or burglary into one's home or business. In other words, the theft must involve property under lock or key, where a breaking or unlawful entry occurred. Property carelessly left out in the open, or property that cannot be guarded or not worth guarding, such as piles of wood, does not warrant amputation if the offender is caught. In some cases, however, the thief may ask forgiveness for his crime. In such cases, he may be spared or shown mercy (an Islamic principle) if he repents and attempts to mend his ways. Thus, amputation is not automatic in every case.

Occasionally, reports of amputations are released by Saudi news sources revealing that certainty of punishment still exists in the Kingdom. One Friday in October, 1998, a Saudi man had his right hand chopped off in the capital city of Riyadh after he was convicted of theft. The offender had a record of theft, having been found guilty of several thefts in the Kingdom. Amputations, like executions in Saudi Arabia, are not the work of local butchers or psychopathic vigilantes conducted in some macabre dungeon or vermin infested cellar. Amputations, as are beheadings, are normally carried out in the center square of town during the noon prayer on the holy day of Friday. The condemned person is brought forward, the verdict read, and the arm stretched out on the surface of a table. The offender's body is turned backward, away from the table. A professional executioner, in the presence of a male physician and nurse, grabs the hand, stretching it away from the wrist.

The executioner with one swift motion severs the hand at the joint of the wrist. The physician quickly bandages the bleeding stump. Such punishment serves not only as a deterrent to onlookers, but allows the offender to return to work or home without serving a lengthy prison term. The question raised is whether such punishment is more barbaric than wasting away in prison for many years.

According to 1997 human rights reports on Saudi Arabian justice and amputations, authorities punish repeated thievery by amputation of the right hand. Excessive amputation has not been imposed since June, 1995, although rare cases of amputation are occurring today. Simply put, amputation is rarely done because of the standard of proof needed, and the requirements that the theft and the offender meet certain standards. You will notice some Huddud crimes are not crimes in Western society. Fornication and adultery, while considered immoral acts by some, are not crimes, unless one of the partners is under the legal age of consent (usually 18 years). Drinking alcohol is a crime only if the person is underage or it is consumed in an inappropriate place, such as a public street or while driving.

Some behaviors, which are often defined as victimless crimes in Western society, are viewed as serious moral deprivation in Islamic societies, resulting in lashing and other extreme punishments. According to information from the State Department, Westerners have spent up to a year in Saudi prisons for alcohol-related offenses, and sentenced to receive 75 or more lashes in lieu of prison for failing a blood test for alcohol.

Arriving passengers displaying signs of intoxication or in possession of alcohol are subject to arrest or deportation. A British visitor found out the hard way what can happen if caught with alcohol. In his 1997 letter, written to the British press in the aftermath of the arrest of the British nurses, he recounts his experiences.

"In October 1994 (while living in Saudi Arabia) during a routine search of my bags, a small quantity of alcohol was found in my water bottle. I kicked myself for forgetting that it was there. I was taken to Mahad al Hazab jail in Western Province. Conditions at the jail were unpleasant but bearable. I was allowed to keep my money to buy food and drinks and, after a bond had been lodged by my company, was released after three days. For my trial on December 26, 1994, I had to return to Western Province with an official interpreter, whose expenses I had to meet. The trial was conducted in a fair manner and the judge sentenced me to 40 lashes. Two months later, I had to travel back to Mahad al Hazab, where I was escorted to the prison and given tea by the prison captain before being taken outside. I had to stand up straight and was flogged on the back with a 5 ft bamboo cane. I was told that my clothes would not be removed, so I wore a thick jumper. There was pain, but it was bearable. No blood was drawn and the marks left on my back weren't serious. I had bruises but no scarring, was escorted back to the prison for the paperwork and asked if I wished to see a doctor. Then I was free to go. I was then approached by the prosecutor and offered a tour of the local gold mine, which I accepted. It was all amicable, with no ill feelings on either side."

—Andrew J Smith, Milton Keynes, Bucks, Daily Mail, 1/10/97

In addition to alcohol, a number of prescription drugs available in other countries are illegal in Saudi Arabia. A visitor is warned about possessing any kind of drug. For instance, captagon (fenetylline hydrochloride), a drug used to treat exhaustion, which is available without a prescription in some countries in Asia, is considered an illegal substance in Saudi Arabia. Americans in Saudi Arabia have received prison sentences of up to 2 1/2 months and 70 lashes for possession of captagon. Before traveling to the kingdom, the traveler is advised to check with the state department or Saudi embassy for drug allowances.

The attempted importation of drugs or controlled substances, even in very small amounts, is a serious offense under Saudi law. But it is more serious if the drug is sold or used in dealing. The traveler arrested and tried for carrying drugs into the country will be punished less severely if the drug is for his own use. Many expatriates have served prison sentences for drug possession or use. The death penalty almost always awaits drug smugglers convicted of a second offense.

A second category of crimes are termed quesas crimes. These crimes normally include murder, arson, and select number of other serious crimes. These are also referred to as retaliation crimes. Quesas crimes include both intentional and unintentional murder. Since these are personal crimes, the victim's family must initiate the prosecution. In other words, murder in Saudi Arabia is generally viewed as a private crime, unless the killing resulted from a robbery by a stranger, in which case it becomes a hadd offense.

In quesas crimes such as intentional murder, the standards of evidence are less demanding, because these crimes have a slim chance of negotiation for blood money or forgiveness. The family of the victim has greater leeway in deciding the fate of the accused because quesas crimes are not bound by the strict guidelines of huddud offenses. This does not mean that the government cannot punish! In both intentional and unintentional murder cases, for example, the government can punish the offender with prison time, but only the victim's male descendants can demand death. Yet intentional murder cannot be proved without the testimony of two eyewitnesses. Islamic law demands that the two eyewitnesses be pious Muslim men. Intentionally can also be proved by a voluntary confession by the accused in open court. Thus, the confession must be given freely and voluntarily. If media reports of the Gilford crime are accurate, the nurses could not be convicted, since they withdrew their confessions.

The third and lowest class is Tazir crimes, which represent an open-ended category or crimes not generally viewed as serious as the other categories. These crimes are analogous to misdemeanors offenses in Western nations. Tazir crimes are acts condemned by law but are not included in the Huddud or Quesas group. Tazir offenses include consumption of pork, false testimony, bribery, and the practice of astrology. Additional examples of tazir offenses are indecency, disorderly conduct, traffic violations, zoning violations and so forth. There is no set punishment for these crimes, allowing judges the ability to exercise wide discretion in administering punishment. Because of the latitude of punishment for traffic violations, visitors often complain that driving a vehicle in the cities of Saudi Arabia has been termed a health hazard, comparable to driving blindfolded in Tijuana, Mexico, on a Saturday night.

In some Islamic nations, Tazir crimes are set by legislative parliament. Each nation is free to establish its own criminal code and there is a great disparity in punishment of some of these crimes. Some additional, common Tazir crimes are: bribery, selling tainted or defective products, treason, usury, and selling obscene pictures. The consumption of alcohol in Egypt is punished much differently than in Iran or Saudi Arabia because they have far different civil laws. Islamic law has much greater flexibility than the Western media portrays.

Punishments for crime are applicable to Muslims and non-Muslims alike. In the late 1970s, a young royal princess was accused of adultery with a commoner and paid the price of execution by a firing squad followed by beheading. The British made a film of the case titled *Death of a Princess*, infuriating the Saudis because of the manner in which Islamic law was portrayed. For years, the film caused a major political rift between the two countries, and as we will see, the Gilford case opened up new wounds.

Punishment is administered according to the concept *"eye for an eye...tooth for a tooth."* Although punishment may have disastrous effects on the offender, it is the by-product of the Islamic principle of God, society, and humans. In other words, punishment serves three purposes: first, it fulfills worship; second, punishment is considered a purification process for society; third, punishment is redemption for the individual. However, of the three, the latter is the least important, for society and God are not expendable. This logic is referred to as utilitarianism, or the philosophy that the interest of society and God takes precedence over the interest of the individual. Interestingly enough, this is very similar to Western thought on punishment, where punishment is designed to protect society from the evil acts of a few.

Saudi Arabia is one of several nations generously employing the death penalty. And because of this, it is a common assumption that death sentences are carried out daily in the Kingdom; however, it was reported that no executions were performed during the five-month period from October 1995 to March 1996. When executions resumed in March 1996, the authorities beheaded 40 men and one woman for murder, 14 men for rape, six men and two women for drug offenses, five men for armed robbery, and one man for witchcraft by the end of the year. Amnesty International substantiates the 1996 account of 69 executions in the kingdom, with another 83 in 1997. Most of those executed were Saudi citizens, all by beheading. There were no reported executions by stoning in 1996. Most of those executed were third world offenders convicted of rape, murder, and drug trafficking.

Death as the ultimate sanction has a storied past in both England and the United States. But in 18th and 19th century England and America, the death penalty was used often and for less severe crimes, such as stealing and forgery. The executions, held in public, were carried out in many different ways. In England, burning at the stake was reserved only for women. Beheading was specifically used for those who had committed treason. Cutting out the stomach and intestines was a common method of doing away with counterfeiters.

Yet hanging was the most common form of execution in the West. On the morning of the death, the doomed prisoner was taken to a wooden scaffold, masked, and hanged by his neck until dead. The body was sometimes left hanging for days for all to see and to be reminded of what awaited them if they succumbed to similar criminal temptations. In those days, and still today in Saudi Arabia, spectators viewed public executions in much the same way we view sporting events today. Women have not escaped the cut of the sword, with at least 11 young women beheaded in Saudi Arabia in the past 10 years. In contrast, United States figures show 56 offenders were executed in 1995, and 74 in 1997 (38 in the state of Texas alone).

However, for the first six months of 1999, Saudi Arabian news reported nearly 50 executions (beheadings) for smuggling drugs, murder, and rape. All offenders were Third World nationals. As for less serious offenses, drinking alcohol in public is punished by jail terms for non-Muslim offenders and whipping and prison for Muslims.

The United States is the only major Western trading partner imposing the ultimate sanction, usually by electrocution, asphyxiation, or lethal injection. Great Britain and Australia avoid such sanctions. The Homicide acts of 1957-65 eliminated capital punishment in Great Britain for murder. China, a major Eastern-trading partner generously employs the death penalty. A bullet to the back of the head, with the family of the offender billed for the cost of the bullet, personalizes the Chinese style of execution.

The interpretation of Islamic law and associated punishment differs between Muslim nations. The strict Taliban government of Afghanistan announced in March, 1998 that two men convicted of homosexuality (sodomy) were buried alive under a wall, which was then bulldozed over them. Under the fundamentalist Islamic regime of that nation, fornication and adultery are taken very seriously.

Neighboring Iran isn't lenient either. Reports of stoning for some offenders are reported in rural areas of the country. Buried to the waist or neck, the condemned man or woman is covered with a white sheet and pelted with rocks which, according to religious law are, "not so large that a person dies after being hit with two of them, nor so small as to be defined as pebbles."

Each judge is free to punish based upon local norms, customs, and is free to fix the punishment that will deter others from crime. Another way to view this is through the standard of proof. If the rigid standard of proof for the other crimes mentioned in the Koran is not met, people are often convicted on a lesser standard of tazir, or chastisement. Less evidence is needed, but the punishments are correspondingly lighter. Penalties may be jail time, corporal punishment, or public shaming such as shaving off one's hair.

A distinction between the three classes of crimes is that huddud and quesas crimes follow the principle of retribution and deterrence, and are deemed more serious, while tazir crimes are concerned with rehabilitation and deterrence with less serious sanctions. Tazir crimes are analogous to misdemeanor offenses.

The Sharia is the will of God as laid down through textual sources. Decisions by judges are a slow process of mediation, and it is not uncommon for judges to argue among themselves before reaching a decision. When a decision is reached, based upon an interpretation of the Sharia, this is referred to as *figh*, or rules formulated by the Muslim jurists.

The Sharia is in direct contrast with Western or man-made law, which seems to change with political climates or wind direction. In other words, law in the Western world is subordinate to man. The Sharia is ordained and cannot be altered by rulers or politics. The fixed standard is difficult for Westerners to grasp, particularly cynical, secular humanists.

Yet, Islam shows compassion for the offender, and its justice system meets International law guidelines of fairness, despite human rights criticisms. In a 1998 law review article (The Georgia Journal of International and Comparative Law), the author cites evidence that the Saudi justice system, when considered in light of the religious convictions underlying Saudi law, applies criminal procedures consistent with international law standards. In other words, fundamentally the law is fair, allowing for standards of proof and due process, even though the law may not meet Western standards or the standards of so called political moralists.

We will learn both nurses in the Gilford case benefited from Sharia compassion in the end. The old adage, "when in Rome, do as the Romans do," should be on anyone's mind when visiting the Kingdom. Appendix E provides additional insight into travel and culture expectations in Saudi Arabia.

3
ALIEN COMPANIONS

Given the culture and display of justice of the Kingdom, why would a westerner venture to a country so restricted, especially a Western female? Reasons vary and often our temptations get the better of us. A popular location for working expatriates is the city of Dhahran, the oil production center of Saudi Arabia. The city is home of Saudi Aramco, the largest oil company in the world. This cosmopolitan city, located on the Persian Gulf, also hosts a military base for more than 2,500 American service personnel. The Saudi economy is almost entirely dependent upon foreign laborers from Egypt, Pakistan, India, and the Philippines. It is the city where the case begins.

The increased number of foreign experts working in Dhahran has brought with them the need for housing, hospitals and schools for their children. Due to foreign industrial interests, particularly oil, many Westerners have found careers in this thriving industrial center with rich opportunities. These adventure-seeking aliens, mostly British and Americans, work in Saudi Arabia as engineers, teachers, medical personnel, or in other skilled occupations.

An attractive, hard working, globe trotting, Australian-born nurse, Yvonne Gilford accepted a tax-free job in the Kingdom. Like many expatriates working in Saudi Arabia, the unmarried nurse hoped to save enough money to retire early and possibly launch into another career. Yvonne Gilford was planning to open her own cake-decorating business in Australia.

A strong and self-reliant woman, she and her brother Frank, the children of a sheep farmer, were brought up on a remote 340,000-acre ranch in Southern Australia. After completing a four-year nursing course, the then 28-year-old worked in Auckland, New Zealand, and eventually migrated to London in 1973. Three years later, Yvonne moved to Johannesburg, South Africa, where she became head nurse of the surgical ward of Lady Dudley Hospital.

In May of 1996, seeking change and additional financial security, she accepted a job at the King Fahd Military Medical Center in Dhahran, Saudi Arabia, a 328-bed teaching hospital that offered a fresh and lucrative career in the conservative Muslim country.

Why does one choose to move to a strange foreign land? For Yvonne, it was the opportunity to save money for her business. For others, it may be an opportunity to experience a different culture while earning a respectable tax-free income; or perhaps an escape from the past, a shattered relationship, or loneliness. Nurses and other professionals accepting work in Saudi Arabia normally sign a one-year contract. Round trip transportation is paid, generous vacations are offered as well as a number of opportunities to earn bonuses.

Yet, there is always a price to pay when relocating to a foreign culture. New relationships must be forged and cultural adjustments made. It was not long after her arrival that Yvonne Gilford sought companionship. Loneliness is particularly painful for single women in a restrictive Muslim society, where over 55 percent of the population is male. The following article written by an Arab journalist points out the plight of women in the conservative kingdom.

Saudi Arabia's restrictions and stiff penalties may not be to every foreign woman's taste, but many find the lure of a tax-free expatriate lifestyle in the kingdom irresistible. Millions of expats have chosen to make a living in the Gulf Arab state despite the drawbacks of a conservative society in which women have to play by a rigid set of rules. The murder trial of British nurses Deborah Parry and Lucille McLauchlan has put the spotlight on Saudi Arabia, the custodian of Islam's holiest sites in Mecca and Medina. Even the often-pugnacious British press, after the initial shock that McLauchlan was sentenced on 23 September to 500 lashes under Islamic law, acknowledged that life in a tax haven can have its drawbacks.

"We may not like Saudi Arabia's idea of justice, but no one is forced to go there... If you choose to work tax-free in a country, then you must live by its customs and laws."

The Sun, a mass-circulation tabloid, reported: Many foreign women in Saudi Arabia enjoy a lifestyle they simply could not afford back home, with perks such as maids, drivers and a house in a compound with swimming pool and tennis court. "For a mother with children, it's a paradise," said a Western woman working at an embassy. "But for a single woman,

*it can be very hard." A 29-year-old Irish ex-flight attendant living in
Jeddah on the Red Sea said many of her married women friends "spend
their day sitting by the pool, or go shopping, and then just eat, eat, eat."
But women are not allowed to drive. "If you don't have a driver, it means
you are reliant on your husband, more so than in any other country. It's
also a hassle for him when he gets back from work to have to drive the wife
to the shops," said the Irish woman. Foreign women are restricted to work
as flight attendants, teachers and nurses, and to abide by rules of segregation. More than 80 percent of nurses in the kingdom's 30 hospitals are
foreigners, a European diplomat said. Nurses are paid around $2,000 a
month on top of free food, accommodation and an annual plane ticket
home. But most of the thousands of nurses live in hospitals rather than
compounds and have a 10 p.m. curfew. They have to sign in every night
or else face a warning. If they are late more than once, they are fired. Life
for single Western women in compounds, some of which can group as
many as 10,000 homes such as the Cordoba compound near Riyadh, can
be far more liberal. "Single women such as nurses are free to do whatever they want within the walls where mixed bathing and bikinis are okay.
Ninety-nine percent of them have boyfriends," said a US national and 10-
year resident of Saudi Arabia.*

*He said home-brew alcohol and parties, both banned, are also com-
mon in the privacy of compounds. Saudi religious police have the right to
check identity cards to ensure non-married couples are not together in
restaurants or cars. Tinted windows on cars are banned to make sure.
"The girls have a good time, but you're always taking a risk," said an ex-
flight attendant, complaining that the penalty is more severe for the
woman.*

*Two nurses, English and Irish, were held for five days after being
caught at night in the car of a Lebanese man, a friend said. They underwent medical examinations that showed they had not had sex but were
still deported. Among other restrictions, the embassy employee said women
cannot try on clothes in boutiques because the staff are men and so
changing rooms are not allowed. They cannot even try on a pair of shoes.
Foreign women also have to abide by a dress code, wearing the black
abaya robe of the Gulf. Most also carry a scarf in their bag, in case they
are shouted at in the street. "I can't drive and I'm not free to walk as I
want in the street," said the Irish woman. "I just don't have the indepen-
dence." Foreign women take the good with the bad in Saudi Arabia.*

—Haro Chakmakjian, Middle East Times, October 5, 1997

Lucille McLauchlan and Deborah Parry arrived in Saudi Arabia in
September of 1996. As with Yvonne Gilford and nearly 5,000 other
medical personnel in Saudi Arabia, they were attracted to the lucrative

opportunities in the oil rich kingdom. The two had different reasons for leaving their countries. For the 32-year-old McLauchlan, it was the need to escape criminal prosecution. The former student nurse-of-the-year from Dundee, Scotland, was discharged from a hospital over allegations she stole a terminally ill patient's credit card, withdrawing funds from her account on several occasions. In debt and in fear of going to jail, she reportedly forged her references enabling her to gain employment in Saudi Arabia and the hope of recapturing financial success and self-respect. It is reported that her father was not aware of her true reasons for trekking to Saudi Arabia.

Deborah Parry's reasons were more personal. Like Gilford, the 39-year-old nurse had an extensive career, working in hospitals in Oxford, Worcester and the King Edward VII hospital in London. Born in Alton, Hampshire County in England, Parry trained as a nurse after winning a scholarship to grammar school. However, her life was marred with tragedy and sadness. When she was 16, her brother Keith died in a motorcycle accident and several weeks after his unfortunate death, her 48-year-old mother drowned while in a boating trip. The tragedy continued eight years later when her father died unexpectedly of a heart attack.

Finding it difficult to cope with the loss of her family, she sought therapy for four years. She then convinced herself that a change of environment was necessary, and Saudi Arabia was the cure. She worked in Saudi Arabia from 1993 to 1995, and decided to return for another hitch in 1996.

The three nurses joined a staff of more than 100 British, Australian and South African nurses. While they made the journey for a variety of reasons, all were in need of friendship in a land not particularly friendly to Western women. It wasn't long after the pair arrived that they became acquainted with the Australian nurse, Yvonne Gilford.

The three reportedly became close friends, often working the same 12-hour shifts in the hospital renal unit, and attending compound's social functions together. They often traveled to the Saudi desert for camping and other activities. The desert is a major playground for expatriates seeking a change from the pressures of compound living. Parry and Gilford had similar backgrounds. Both were compassionate nurses with distinguished work records, a flair for adventure, and a need for change.

Working in a conservative culture, with its strict legal and social codes, brought the nurses closer together. Just how close the pair became is unknown, but allegations by the Saudi police suggested the trio was involved in an intense lesbian relationship. When people are estranged from their friends and family, the need for a caring companion can result in sexual relationships, whether homosexual or heterosexual.

According to a nurse who worked at the hospital, "It was common knowledge Yvonne was a lesbian." Both the Parry and Gilford families vehemently reject such allegations that either of the nurses was lesbian; after all, Parry reportedly enjoyed two long-term relationships with men, and Gilford conducted an affair with a South African businessman for nearly twenty years.

Further assertions arose that Yvonne Gilford had a more sinister side to her personality. She often lent money to co-workers and used a Filipino henchman to intimidate those who owed her cash. It was reported that McLauchlan owed Gilford a considerable amount of money, increasing speculation that money was the basis for the argument and a motive in the killing. Yet another twist is that compound security guards who allegedly operated a moneylending business as well, had warned Gilford not to interfere with their lucrative sideline.

On December 10, 1996, the three nurses gathered for a Christmas party at the residential compound. Entertainment is widely available in the claustrophobic environment of the compound, with taverns and discos available to the expatriates. And, for the most part, the Saudis ignore the partying expatriates as long as they confine their activities to the compound. The compounds are patrolled by security officers to assure curious Saudi citizens are not exposed to Western life inside the high stucco walls.

As the evening wore on, a quarrel erupted between the three. It is unclear why they were in dispute, but there was obviously tension, noticeable to the others attending the party. The events that transpired afterwards would forever change the lives of many and involve the governments of three powerful nations.

4
MURDER AND MOTIVE

Yvonne Gilford failed to report for her scheduled shift on the morning of December 12, 1996. It was not like her to be late. Several calls to her room went unanswered, causing concern by her supervisor Desalian Marks, that she may have had an accident. It was extremely unlikely Yvonne simply forgot to report to work, and if she were running late, she would surely report the delay.

Since Lucille McLauchlan was a friend and co-worker of Gilford, she was asked by Marks if she had any information as to why Gilford failed to show for her shift. Her answer was that she did not know. It was later revealed that McLauchlan, along with other expatriates, was in Gilford's apartment the night before watching videos.

Sensing something was wrong, McLauchlan and several other co-workers immediately went to Gilford's apartment. Upon arrival, security officers were already at the scene. As the nurses stood watching, an officer knocked on the door, but failed to get a response. Fearing an accident, the officers entered the unit with a passkey and were shocked when they discovered Gilford's lifeless body on the bedroom floor.

A blanket covered her head, and concealed underneath the blanket was her shirt and brassiere pulled up around her neck. White socks and a small pillow—all stained with blood—were lying next to her head. Her pale body displayed puncture wounds, bruises and blood-soaked clothing. Her eyes were in a fixed stare reflecting the horror of her final moments of life. Large blood stains covered the floor surrounding her body.

The scene of any murder is particularly gruesome. Some victims are mutilated beyond recognition; throats slashed, eyes gouged from their sockets, genitals removed and stuffed in the mouths of the victim. Other scenes are less bloody. In such cases, the victim may have been poisoned or strangled. And the manner of killing is often indicative of motive and the mental state of the offender. The bloodier and more disorganized the crime scene, the greater the likelihood that passion was the primary motive, and more likely that evidence will be recovered at the scene. The position of the body and method of killing are crucial to the investigation because some offenders will intentionally or unintentionally leave clues at the scene. In police investigative parlance, these clues are called "trademarks."

Whoever committed the murder did not want to see her even after death. It is as if the killer(s) were embarrassed or even shocked by their loathsome act. The brutal scene hinted that the killer or killers attempted an undoing of the crime. Undoing is a killer's way of expressing remorse or blotting out the crime. It is as if to say, *"Oh my God... what have I done, I am so sorry... I don't want to look at her."* These trademarks are associated with murders where the victim and offender had or were having a relationship, such as in murders resulting from domestic violence or a steaming relationship turned ugly.

At 8:30 on the morning of December 12, 1996, security officers notified the Dhahran police of the murder. A murder on Saudi soil, including the Western residential compounds, is the investigative responsibility of the nearest Saudi police authorities. And expatriates are subject to arrest for crimes regardless of their nationality and location of the crime. Just because the victim and offender happen to be Westerners or non-Muslims does not protect them from investigation or arrest.

Shortly after Gilford's body was discovered, the police arrived at the apartment. They did what police are supposed to do in cases like this. They surveyed the scene, took photos, and searched for crucial evidence that might lead to the killer(s). A portion of the preliminary police report (# 21/13/1369/S), dated 12 December 1996, provides a summary of the initial investigation:

The deceased was found lying on the floor of her room—her head was on the East Side and her legs were on the west, close to and on the east side of the bed. She was wearing a shirt with designs on it together with brief shorts. The shirt was pulled up towards the top of her body. There were several stabbing injuries on various parts of the body and one of those was on the back of the right thigh. There was also an incised wound on the right side of the waist as well as several other stabs of various sizes on the back of the deceased. There was a blanket over head. When the blanket was removed, we found beige trousers belonging to the deceased, a brassiere, white socks and a small pillow, all stained with blood. There were several stabs on the left front as well as in the middle of the deceased's neck. There was an incised wound on the forehead and blows to the right eye, nose and mouth which were covered with blood... apart from some blood splotches around the dead body and near the kitchen sink, no other traces of violence or resistance was seen. The door and the windows in the room showed no signs of damage.

As with any major crime scene investigation, a search for evidence and witnesses was undertaken immediately. The body of Yvonne Gilford was taken to Dammam Central Hospital for an autopsy, a standard practice in Saudi Arabia and other countries when the circumstances surrounding a death are suspicious and there is a need to determine the cause of death.

Especially with a murder case, co-workers, friends, and other acquaintances are considered leads or even suspects. Police in a murder investigation focus on the victim's associations, for it is often intimates or acquaintances that are most often responsible for causing another's death. In fact, most murder victims die at the hands of an acquaintance, relative, former or current loved one. It therefore would seem unlikely that a stranger killed Gilford, particularly since no evidence of a forced intrusion or breaking was identified. The apartment was remarkably clean, no blood spattered walls or furniture, broken glassware, or ransacking commonly associated with violent struggles and disorganized killings.

Gilford's ground floor apartment was only a short distance from the compound security post, but strangely no one at the post heard or saw anything. The scene seemed intact, as if whoever killed her took the time to clean the scene or remove evidence. Equally as important as solving a murder is the need to preserve the reputation and competence of a police agency.

Regardless of whether the murder is committed in Saudi Arabia, England, or Brentwood, California, all eyes are on the police to arrest those responsible and to do it quickly. Murder is a crime which severely undermines the social fabric of a society.

Sex, revenge, jealousy, rage, a cover-up for another crime, a sudden argument turned physical, political, financial gain, and thrill are motives for murder. Some murders are planned, such as terrorist bombings or assassinations. Many victims in these cases are often unknown to the offender. Murders committed by intimates may also be planned, yet many are spontaneous, the result of a heated dispute, bordering on sex, jealousy or money problems.

The location of the crime scene, the lifestyle of the victim, choice of weapon, the extent and type of injuries to the body suggest motive as well as style. Some murder victims actually invite their own death by their lifestyles and shady associations. The adage: "If you swim with sharks you're liable to be bitten" holds true for those who undertake risky activities or associate with known hoodlums.

The murder of Yvonne Gilford suggested a killing following an argument or altercation, by someone known by her, or at the very least familiar with her lifestyle. The death patterned a spontaneous domestic slaying triggered by some stressful event, such as an argument fueled by jealousy or anger.

Why such a conclusion? The autopsy report (the report was later criticized by outside experts as being incomplete) revealed Gilford was not sexually violated; no semen stains or pubic hairs were found on her body; no evidence of alcohol or other drugs was found in her system. The apartment was not ransacked, thus suggesting that whoever committed the murder was not searching for money or other valuables.

No evidence of pre-planning, which can give insight into the offender(s) mind, was apparent. Gilford's shirt was pulled over her head to cover her face during the commission of the crime, indicating some level of spontaneity, as opposed to bringing a blindfold or tape to cover the victim's eyes (indicating pre-planning).

The violent, frenzied slashing injuries all over the victim's body indicate rage and familiarity with the victim, or perhaps a need to depersonalize the victim. A murder with a knife causing injuries to a certain part of the body such as the chest area suggests the victim was unconscious or did not struggle. This was not the case with Yvonne Gilford, for she sustained wounds all over her body, and had apparently put up a fight.

A subsequent police report indicated the deceased was "holding some hair of light color and varying length. One hair was approximately 9 cms long." Grasping of hair is often associated with strangulation or suffocation, where the struggling victim reaches out at anything to prevent the assault. Gilford, in her final moments of life, fought with her attacker(s) as the pillow was pressed against her mouth. In her vain struggle, she grabbed the attacker's hair.

Western media reports erroneously indicated Gilford received between four and thirteen stab wounds (depending on which news release you read). However, the autopsy report indicated over twenty stab wounds on the back, neck, face, head, chest, abdomen, arms and legs; and that many wounds were defense wounds, lacerations or surface wounds on the arms and hands resulting from the victim's futile attempts to ward off the attacker.

In the final moments of terror, Gilford faced her attacker, struggling in vain to stay alive; a series of stab wounds on her chest, neck, forehead, and stomach, with one stomach wound five centimeters long. Stab wounds on the back, ranging from one to three centimeters long suggested Gilford twisted around in her attempt to resist the grasp of her killer.

Many stabs reported in the 17-page autopsy report were identified as superficial wounds, supporting the belief that Gilford struggled fiercely, forcing the killer to pursue her more and more. In other words, the killer or killers had difficulty applying direct wounds on the body. But a knife wasn't the instrument of death. Gilford's body had a number of bruises and contusions, possibly from being pushed and hit, and thrown to the floor. Drops of blood under the right eye and an abrasion on the nose hinted at a blunt object used to incapacitate her.

On the floor, a metal teapot was identified as the blunt object used to strike Gilford. A search revealed the alleged murder weapon, a standard kitchen bread knife found in Gilford's kitchen drawer. The nineteen centimeter blade was apparently wiped clean and in good shape.

A major bruise over the right eye extending to the right side of the forehead and upper part of the nose was detailed in the report. Abrasions were found on the stomach, back, and neck. Then there was the pillow. Why was a pillow lying next to her body? Perhaps it was used to quiet her screams for help.

The forensic medical specialist Dr. Abdulmonaim Abou Al-Fatouh Abou Al-Malati concluded that Yvonne Gilford's death resulted from *"... stab wounds, which penetrated the heart, lungs, liver, spleen, and right kidney, causing heavy bleeding and pneumothorax in the chest and dramatic collapse of breathing and blood circulation."* Absent from the coroner's conclusion was the use of a pillow.

The seriousness of murder varies depending upon the manner of the crime and the mind of the accused. The most serious murder in any society is intentional killing, or murder committed with planning or malice. Murders of this type are the result of terrorist activities, profit motives (robbery), pleasure, or to conceal other crimes. Some murders are unintentional or without malice, such as those resulting from sudden quarrels or disputes. However, murder is primarily a passion crime, usually fueled by some triggering, often spontaneous event between persons known by each other.

Any violence directed toward another usually results from some triggering event. An intrusion into someone's personal space, such as cutting into another's right of way on a highway, has resulted in murder. Discovering your spouse or loved one is bedding down with your best friend, or a dispute over the ownership of a bottle of brew can justify some to fly into a rage and kill.

The primary link to intimate relationship murder is possessiveness. Murders resulting from this motive include infidelity by one of the partners, sudden termination of a relationship, or jealousy over the partner's attention to someone else or other activity. What happened to Yvonne Gilford occurs every day across the globe. One fact is clear: whenever a murder is investigated, the crime scene must be preserved and potential friends and associates of the victim carefully questioned. Finding a motive will answer many questions, and placing someone at the scene before the murder is significant in the overall Investigation.

Who killed Yvonne Gilford? Was it the nurses, as argued by the police? While the police have their theory, there have been other arguments as to Gilford's sudden and brutal demise. Five theories are explored in the following pages. The last chapter will revisit the arguments and evidence as to whom may have killed Yvonne Gilford.

Shattered Lesbian Relationship Theory: The Police Version

The police believe Deborah Parry, with the assistance of Lucille McLauchlan, murdered Yvonne Gilford. The murder was committed in the early morning hours of December 12, 1996. The motive for the killing was sexual, resulting from a dispute over Parry breaking off a lesbian relationship with Gilford. The police investigation revealed McLauchlan was one of the last persons to see Gilford alive, and may have exceptional insight into her death. However, Gilford is known to have other friends. Carolyn Pavlowski, a polish plaster technician at the hospital, reportedly visited Gilford the same evening, just a few hours before McLauchlan. Yet, the focus of the investigation began with the questioning and subsequent arrest of Lucille McLauchlan along with Deborah Parry on December 19, 1996.

The police theory pits Parry as the primary killer and McLauchlan as an accessory to murder. Parry killed Gilford after the two fought over Parry's desire to end a lesbian relationship. During the argument, Gilford phoned McLauchlan, asking her to come to her apartment to help intervene in the dispute. The three talked for a couple of hours; the argument erupted again, with Gilford taking a kitchen knife in an attempt to stab Parry.

There was a struggle, resulting in Gilford being stabbed several times by Parry, with McLauchlan holding Gilford, and placing a pillow over her mouth. McLauchlan and Parry cleaned the apartment and rearranged the furniture. As an afterthought, they took Gilford's bankcard and left the apartment.

Some of Parry and McLauchlan's co-workers believe they were guilty of the murder, but not of having a lesbian relationship. In an interview with the Irish Times reported on October 1, 1997, Rosemary Kidman, a friend of Deborah Parry, said the nurse had been acting strangely in the week after Gilford was stabbed to death. She believed Deborah Parry and

Lucille McLauchlan killed Ms. Gilford. Kidman, who worked in the same hospital, was quoted in a news saying: *"I feel they are very much guilty and everyone at the hospital feels that also, over there in Dhahran. And we took a lot to come to that."*

Kidman stated Parry told her that she had a falling out with Gilford six weeks before the murder, and there had been some ill feelings between the two. It was also reported in the press that Gilford boozed up on local firewater called Sid.

Catherine Wall, a nurse who worked with Gilford, McLauchlan and Parry, suggested Parry may be responsible for the murder of Yvonne Gilford. In a 1998 British television interview titled *Death of a Sister,* Wall states that on the day of the murder, Parry described the stabbing of Gilford even before information was released about how the death occurred. How, wondered Wall, did Parry know anything about the murder details so soon when no else did?

After the murder, Wall observed scratches on Parry's arms and hands resembling the type one would normally get in a struggle. When questioned about the scratches, Parry dismissed the injuries as cat scratches.

Even Parry's hairdresser offered an observation about Parry's possible involvement in Gilford's death. Ann Fitzpatrick, interviewed on the same British Station, noticed a number of hairs missing from Parry's head. It appeared to Fitpatrick that someone *"pulled Debbie's hair out in spots."* According to Fitzpatrick, Parry told her she received a bad haircut as an explanation as to why so much of her hair was missing. Missing hair and scratches on the arm suggest some type of struggle, but the question remains is this enough to convict absent a confession?

Loanshark Retaliation theory:
Accusations surfaced after the murder that Yvonne Gilford was a loan shark. Loan sharks loan money at high interest rates, higher than banks and other lending institutions. The need for a quick loan, or those without the credit to borrow from established lending institutions, make loan-sharking a profitable business. Borrowing from a shark is a risk; those unable to repay the debt, or who are late on payments, are subject to intimidation and physical punishment.

According to a Briton who resided in Saudi Arabia for fifteen years and occasionally worked as a pharmacist at the King Fahd Military Medical Complex, Gilford was a loan shark. She allegedly charged 25% interest for loaning money, and if the borrower was late, an additional 25 % was added to the debt. She allegedly used Filipinos, who were trained in martial arts, to intimidate and threaten people who failed to repay debts on time. In 1997, the British pharmacist provided a statement to the defense team (February 18, 1997) concerning her knowledge of Gilford's character and alleged loan-sharking operation.

"The first night I was introduced to Yvonne Gilford, I was told by another lady present at the table in the social club that it would be unwise to be particularly friendly with Yvonne because of her reputation. During the remainder of the evening and during conversation I learned that Yvonne was a loan shark and this was frowned upon by the Western community... it was also common knowledge that Gilford was a lesbian... I have no direct knowledge of her ever lending money. I can only tell you what I was told."

The Briton's statements, if based on fact, shed additional credence to the loan sharking and lesbian theory. But additional statements suggest even more sinister evidence against Gilford. The pharmacist's son, who attended boarding school in England, visited Saudi Arabia while on holiday. While in Dhahran, he met a friend, a Filipino karate instructor. The pharmacist's statement about what her son told her reads:

"He relayed to me that he had been approached by the instructor who asked if he wished to earn any extra money while he was out on holiday. My son thought that he was asking him to teach Judo or martial arts to other pupils. However, my son told me that he was being asked to lean on people on behalf of Yvonne Gilford and that he was being asked to approach various people to intimidate and threaten them in view of the fact they owed Yvonne sums of money that they had borrowed from her... My son told me he was asked to work for two nights for a fee of 500 Riyals (about 100 pounds)..."

Lucille McLauchlan's outstanding criminal background was common knowledge among the other nurses. Some wondered how she got hired with a criminal past. As implied by the pharmacist, *"It was always a topic of discussion amongst nurses in the social club."* This leads to the essence of the theory. Could it be Lucille McLauchlan, indebted to Gilford and suffering from money woes, who killed Yvonne Gilford with the assistance of another party?

According to other expatriates, since those employed by the Saudi government are not always paid on time or on a regular basis, money lending in Saudi Arabia is a common practice. Borrowing from other expatriates rather than dealing with outside institutions is oftentimes easier. Speculation arose that both Parry and McLauchlan, recent arrivals to Saudi Arabia, were short of finances and possibly borrowing money from Gilford.

It was claimed that McLauchlan owed Gilford a small fortune in unpaid loans. It was further claimed by other expatriates working at the hospital that both McLauchlan and Parry had borrowed money from loan sharks at another base, and decided to pay the other sharks first, leaving them with no money to repay Gilford. The two British roommates may have paid Gilford a visit about their debt, or the need for further funds, leading to an altercation and killing.

Greed and Snitch Theory:

This theory, although supported by less evidence, reasons other miscreants operated a loan-sharking and prostitution business in the compound. Gilford knew too much, was interfering, and had to be eliminated. Those others may have been Filipinos who obviously had knowledge of the alleged loan-sharking business Gilford operated, or maybe the Filipinos were working with security guards in loan-sharking and other unscrupulous activities occurring at the compound. According to some expatriates, evidence of security guards *"trading money for sex with Filipino women"* was common. As the theory suggests, perhaps Yvonne Gilford knew about such activities and threatened to report them unless cut in on the action. The Filipinos may have attempted to reason with her and failed, or Gilford and the others were conspirators, who simply had a falling out over division of profits.

It is not unusual for conspirators or partners in crime to turn against each other. Greed has a way of turning people against each other, especially the morally weak or ambitious. It is not beyond the realm of imagination that if an illegal scheme was going on within the compound, any threat to snitch could prove disastrous for the informant. Survival of many is more important than the preservation of one.

Fatal Attraction Theory:

In 1994, Maria Guzman, a married Filipino nurse was murdered at the King Fahd Military Medical Complex. No one was charged in her murder; her husband was a suspect, but reportedly was somewhere else at the time of the murder. However, he died under suspicious circumstances several days after his arrest while in custody. According to Sharon Markula, a former nurse at the medical center now living in Brisbane, Australia, the modus operandi of her murder was similar to that of Gilford's.

In an interview with Scotland's *Daily Record* in 1997, Markula, who worked at the hospital for two years, said that Gilford, a fellow Australian, had been harassed by security guards in the weeks before her death as had Mrs. Guzman. She said both women had received large amounts of back pay before their murder. Both had been beaten and stabbed; Guzman, a Filipino, was strangled; Gilford was suffocated and stabbed. Markula claimed that a security guard had "gone missing" shortly after each death. "She (Guzman) was living in fear because her room had been broken into twice," said Markula.

The *Daily Record* went on to say:

"She was terrified because only the security guards had a copy of the room key. Someone had got in and left a cigarette butt in her kitchen. It was like a calling card to warn her she was being watched. The same thing happened to Yvonne and she was keeping a diary of the break-ins and weird phone calls before she died."

Allegations were made that a male security guard whose affection was rejected, might have killed her. Several nurses at the compound described how a male security guard pestered Gilford in the weeks before she was killed. Although the security post was only a few meters from Gilford's room, none of the security guards admitted hearing cries for help or the sound of a fight. The most sinister revelation is that five guards were arrested days before the two Britons. All were discharged and have since disappeared. Why were they arrested? Where did they go?

This theory posits that a security officer was after Gilford and may be a suspect of the crime. In McLauchlan's statement to the police, she stated that Gilford complained a male security guard was *"peeping in at her."* A possible scenario under this theory is that a guard came to Gilford's unit (the guard would have known her lifestyle and working hours) seeking a business deal, or sexual encounter, but a struggle evoked resulting in Gilford's death. A man's bracelet was found in Gilford's room, which could have belonged to the same guard, or another male intruder. Based on the crime scene and other evidence, it is safe to say that whoever killed Yvonne Gilford knew her well.

The Rogue Nurse Theory:

Some persons close to the case suggest the theory that Lucille acting alone killed Yvonne Gilford. Why the suggestion? It is known that nurses often had keys to each other's rooms. Under this theory, Lucille McLauchlan went to Gilford's room while Gilford was away. Her intentions were to remove any valuables or money, and get out before Gilford's return. In the compound society, particularly among friends, it is common to know of each other's whereabouts, and we know from later accounts that Lucille had a history of larceny, which would explain her surreptitious behavior. In any event, this theory proposes that while Lucille was rummaging through Yvonne's possessions, Yvonne returned unexpectedly. Naturally, the explanation offered by Lucille was unacceptable to Yvonne resulting in an argument followed by a tussle.

Burglary offenders, who enter another's home for the purposes of committing a theft, often turn violent upon discovery. Likewise, victims of these intrusions may become violent upon discovery of the intrusion. In this scenario, Lucille killed Yvonne Gilford for fear or actual threats that Yvonne would report the unlawful entry to the police. Lucille may have summoned Deborah Parry to assist her in the cleanup of the apartment. Since was Parry was a friend, and by getting her involved, she could reduce her culpability in the murder, or possibly spread responsibility if caught. Lucille left the apartment with Yvonne's bankcard, and subsequently laundered her clothes to remove any evidence. Lucille was observed laundering her clothes at a time shortly after the murder. It is possible Deborah was ignorant of Lucille's possession of the bankcard, but if she did, went along with the theft.

To sum up the several theories, it is clear that a number of combinations of *"who done its"* can be fashioned. Maybe Debbie Parry acted alone, or maybe another expatriate committed the murder. But it is plain that under Western justice systems, the more theories presented, the more doubt one is able to be cast on certain parties. In other words, the crux of any defense is to raise the question of doubt. The more doubt raised, the more likely an acquittal. These theories make the job of a defense attorney much easier. However, we are in Saudi Arabia not in the courtrooms of London or Los Angeles.

5
ARREST AND CONFESSION

After the death of Yvonne Gilford, a number of her associates were under suspicion; the police interviewed many nurses at the compound. They reportedly lined up the staff in the hospital auditorium looking for clues or injuries associated with the murder of Gilford. In final analysis, roommates Lucille McLauchlan and Debbie Parry were at the top of the list. It was known McLauchlan was in Gilford's apartment a few hours before the murder. The three were friends, working in the same unit, and often socializing together at the compound social club. McLauchlan and Gilford bought a bicycle together several weeks before the murder. Rumors circulated among expatriates at the compound that the three were lesbians; although this allegation was never established as fact, it was a constant source of conversation among co-workers, fueled later by the police during the intensive investigation process.

The police moved quickly, questioning McLauchlan at lunchtime on 12 December 1996, about four hours after the murder was discovered. The questioning lasted about half an hour, focusing on her knowledge of Gilford, and the relationship between Gilford and Parry. The questioning was more of a "feeling out" process, whereby the police look for nervousness and other clues indicating possible knowledge on the part of the unsuspecting interviewee.

The next day, on 13 December, at approximately 6:00 p.m., McLauchlan was summoned to the Dhahran Police Station and questioned for three hours. The questioning became more intense, focusing on her relationship with Gilford, and why neither of them was married. Under the culture of the Kingdom, unmarried women raise suspicions.

The police questioned McLauchlan about why she had a key to Gilford's room. It is a common practice for nurses in the tightly knit compound to have keys to each other's rooms in the event one is locked out. Questioning continued on December 14, when McLauchlan was called again to the Dhahran police station. She was checked for scratches and bruises (none found) and questioned for over two and a half-hours. It was becoming painfully clear she was a prime suspect in the murder.

On the morning of December 15, McLauchlan was told to report to the police station for a fourth time. The questioning became more aggressive, with suggestions that the two women were having an affair. The police persistently asked why she was in Gilford's apartment the night before the murder. After three hours, she was allowed to leave. At 9:00 p.m. that evening, the police searched her apartment.

"Shut up and be quiet," was the response McLauchlan received when she asked why her apartment was searched. The police took a pair of pajamas and a towel. Taking such evidence suggests the police were searching for hairs or fibers and possibly bloodstains from Yvonne Gilford. These searching methods also suggest that the police were possibly intimidating the nurses, or preparing them for the next phase of interrogation. Whether the police found any incriminating evidence or not, they were making it clear that their attention was focusing squarely on the nurses.

During the early days of the investigation, the hospital became a command center for the police. Command centers are central locations in which the police launch their investigations. That evening, the police took McLauchlan's fingerprints. It was becoming evident the police were concentrating on Lucille as the primary suspect in the killing of Yvonne Gilford.

In addition to her association with McLauchlan, the police suspected Parry was involved with the murder because of the manner with which Parry was affected by the killing. After the killing, Parry had gone to the employee hospital shortly afterwards for anti depressant medication. In other words, the Saudi police earmarked her as a possible suspect because of her reaction to the murder.

The police made it clear to other staff members that the nurses were key suspects in the murder. The police were monitoring the two women. Desalin Marks, McLauchlan's supervisor, told McLauchlan and Parry to inform her of their "whereabouts at all times," further evidence that the police were focusing strongly on the nurses. Like a snake poised to strike, the police were closing in, waiting for additional evidence, or a wrong move. It was just a matter of time.

Yet, surprisingly, there was a pause in the harassment. The next three days brought a reprieve from the constant police badgering and insinuations. Neither nurse was called to the police station, but it was an uneasy feeling, like a calm breeze before the onslaught of a violent storm. McLauchlan and Parry were exhausted after finishing a 12-hour shift; compounding their exhaustion was the stress of the investigation, and the constant suspicion of their involvement. Obviously, they were in no position to leave the country, and even if they tried, they surely would be detained. But, surprisingly, there is no evidence that the nurses attempted to contact anyone from the British embassy regarding their predicament prior to their arrest.

Understandably, both nurses were apprehensive and paranoid since they had to inform their supervisor of every movement; after finishing their shift at 7:15 a.m., the nurses left the hospital at 8:00 a.m. taking a cab into Alkhobar to do some shopping. Unknown to either, it would be the last trip they would make as free women for the next 16 months.

The coiled snake patiently poised was now ready to strike. Once in town, McLauchlan and Parry split up, with McLauchlan conducting business at the Arab National Bank, and Parry entering the nearby Al-Shola mall. Reports conflict as to how the girls were actually arrested, but reliable sources close to the investigation state that the police followed both of the girls into the shopping precinct. Parry went off to a pet shop to buy some cat food and Lucille went to the bank. Lucille placed Gilford's card in the machine, thus alerting the bank manager, who had been previously alerted that Gilford's card was being used.

The manager found Lucille in his branch just about to telex money home. The manager took her into his office and he said, *"You just used my cash machine; can I ask you which card you used?"* Lucille took Yvonne's card out and handed it to the bank manager.

He asked for identification and she gave him her hospital pass and he said, *"This card is not yours it does not match your identification."* McLauchlan said, *"I'm sending some money home for a friend."* The bank manager reportedly replied, *"I don't think that is quite true."*

It is reported that McLauchlan basically fell apart in the office and got out a pack of cigarettes. The police came in and she was taken to the station. Meanwhile, As Deborah Parry walked in the mall, a man approached her in a thobe. *"Come with me,"* he commanded. *"I was very frightened at this point,"* added Parry. *"No explanation was given to me and I was told to shut up when I asked where I was going."*

Parry was also quickly ushered to an awaiting car and taken to the Dhahran police station. She did not know if McLauchlan was still at the mall or had been taken to the station. *"My shopping and handbag was taken away from me. I was so frightened as I cannot speak Arabic and no one told me why I was there or what was going to happen to me."*

McLauchlan describes her arrest differently. She stated that she was arrested in the parking lot of the mall, where three men in gutras and thobes, and a man in trousers and jacket told her to "Get in the car." Another man grabbed her hands, forcing them behind her back, applying handcuffs. Both nurses were taken in separate cars to the police station.

At the station, the women were separated during the interrogation. Parry was taken into a room with several officers and questioned. Six police officers encircled her, and she was very frightened. She was told that she had killed Yvonne Gilford.

"They said I was having a lesbian relationship with her and that I was a very bad person." Sobbing with fear, Parry insisted she had not killed Yvonne Gilford, who was a friend and colleague. The police believed otherwise; every time Parry tried to speak she was told, *"Shut up, you son of a bitch."*

The intense questioning continued with Parry crying and shaking. *"The police would not let me have a drink or use the toilet,"* she said. One of the officers named Major Hamed, the only English-speaking officer, directed the questioning. *"He kept coming in and out of the room pulling my hair and slapping my face... calling me a son of a bitch,"* she continued. Parry was told to remove her abaya; the police touched her breasts and rubbed her crotch.

The police kept insinuating that Parry had had sex with Gilford. She said they seemed to enjoy making sexual suggestions about the alleged relationship between the two nurses. *"One of the policemen was licking his lips and asking me who initiated the sex with 'you and your girlfriend, Yvonne.'"* Parry kept denying she was a lesbian, but the officers persisted, *"No, you son of a bitch, you are the killer and used to lick Yvonne until you killed her."*

Major Hamed, the one who questioned Parry, also questioned McLauchlan and told her she had had Gilford's bankcard and showed her the handbag taken from her outside the bank. Hamed took a green bankcard out of the handbag and 5000 Riyals, calling Lucille a *"thief and harlot."* Lucille denied having the bankcard, stating she only had 3000 Riyals, not 5000.

The pressure to get a confession from Lucille McLauchlan was intense. The police believed Parry was the real killer, but decided to target McLauchlan. The events that took place that morning are reflected in her statement:

"Hamed slapped my face and sat next to me with his hand on my thigh. He told me I would write a statement saying I stole Yvonne's bankcard after Debbie killed her. He told me if I refused I would be hit. I refused and stated he could not do this. Hamed stated that he could do

anything he wanted. The police were the law in Saudi Arabia, and Islam ruled and British were trash... He told me I was a British harlot who meant nothing here."

The police kept pressuring her to confess. McLauchlan asserted that the police threats were escalating into sexual harassment.

"The other 5 policemen were all sitting around me and Hamed told me that one of them thought I was pretty. Hamed pulls me up off the chair and I am told to take my abaya off. I refused. I am slapped several times across the face by Hamed and another policeman pulls my hair from behind me. I take my abaya off. I am crying now and asking them to stop hitting me. The handcuffs are put back on behind my back. I have ankle chains put around my ankles. I am not allowed to sit down. I have to stand near a wall in the office. Everyone is talking in Arabic except Hamed who talks to me in English. I am refused permission to have a drink of water or use the toilet. I also feel nauseated I am so frightened."

The police needed a confession, a crucial requirement under Islamic law. This type of justice is referred to as confessional-based justice. Confessions are viewed as big bonuses for the police. Careers are enhanced with a confession, and of course cases are closed. From another point of view, a confession is viewed as a cleansing, a form of repentance. If you confess all will be fine, even if it means losing your head.

McLauchlan was repeatedly told that if she confessed, she would be given water and permission to use the toilet.

"Told if I write a statement I can sit down and use the toilet. I refuse to write a statement. The policemen take turns in pushing my head back against the wall with the palms of their hands against my forehead. They stamp on my feet every 10–15 minutes. Hamed and another policeman feel and poke my breasts. Colonel Zahrani puts his hands between my legs and laughs when I start crying. One of the policemen has a plastic spatula type thing. He uses it to kill flies. He hit me on my arms and the top of my legs with it until I stop crying. I am refused permission to sit down for what seemed like hours. I am desperate for the toilet. Refused permission to go. Comments are continuously made about how pretty I am and would I like to have a policeman's baby? If I cry I am slapped across the face and my hair is pulled, my feet are stamped on, my breasts and private parts are felt, so I stop crying. I literally beg to go to the toilet and also for a drink of water."

Saudi police are relentless when it comes to getting a confession. If you do not confess the first time, attempts are made over and over until you do.

"Most prisoners confess in the end. It's the thing to do—if you don't confess you will not get to see your embassy—they can make you say anything." This was the conclusion of one American national released

from a Saudi prison in 1997, who experienced first hand confessional justice. The American shared a cell with the British nurses for several weeks.

By this time McLauchlan had been awake for nearly 19 hours, and had worked a 12-hour shift just prior to her arrest at the bank. Imagine the stress created through the relentless questioning and denial of basic creature comforts. Her statement continues as follows:

"The six policemen continue to laugh at me and make comments via Major Hamed about my face and body. I am asked details about my sex life and informed that one of the policemen is also a doctor and if I do not write a statement which Major Hamed tells me he will help me to write, I will be taken to another room and locked in the room with this policeman and stripped. He would also have sex with me as would all the rest of the policemen take it in turns to rape me. He tells me no one will ever believe me if I told them as the police are the law in Saudi Arabia. Major Hamed is standing against me when he states this and it is very obvious he has an erection. I beg him to let me go to the toilet. He refuses."

During the ordeal, Lucille McLauchlan tells Michael Dark, one of the lawyers representing her, of wetting herself; the officers laugh and make fun of her condition. Feeling ashamed and humiliated, McLauchlan removes her trousers and panties. She is told to put her abaya on and is finally permitted to use the toilet. The only garment worn under the abaya is her T-shirt. Upon returning from using the toilet, McLauchlan is told to remove her abaya, and recounts the following:

"I am told to sit next to a desk and Hamed continues to tell me what to write. He keeps going in and out of the office. When he comes in the office he tells me that Debbie killed Yvonne. I was a witness and I stole her bankcard. I write a statement to this effect. I am told that because Yvonne is a Christian and Debbie and me are also, the murderer of Yvonne is no problem as only Muslims are important in Saudi. He tells me over and over again that if I cooperate I will be home in two to three weeks. He keeps promising this. At this stage I would do or write anything to stop the physical, sexual and psychological abuse..."

"If you cooperate and be a good girl no one will touch you or fuck you." McLauchlan reports that the threat of sexual abuse is becoming more real. She is told that one of the police officers is *"just itching to fuck her."*

During the interrogation process, McLauchlan reports being befriended by one of the police officers. He is described as a fat man who washed her clothes. At one point she had diarrhea, and the fat officer washed her pants and joggers. He also reportedly told her to be careful of Officer Hamad.

"He is a big problem, be a good sister," warned the officer in obvious reference to Hamad. *"Do what he tells you."* While McLauchlan

feels the officer felt sorry for her, this also may be interpreted as a technique to get her to confess.

This approach is termed the good cop, bad cop approach to interrogation. One officer is threatening and the other is kind. The kind officer appeals to the sensitivity of the offender, acts as a protector from the other more hostile interrogator. A show of kindness may cause the arrested person to give in to the interrogation.

It is now December 20, 1996, one day after her arrest. McLauchlan has been without sleep for 32 hours. Until December 25, 1996, she is shuttled back and forth from the Dammen prison to the police station in Daharan, where she allegedly undergoes abuse and threats of rape. The entire ordeal is designed to get a confession at any cost. She is continually told that if she confesses she will be home in 2-3 weeks.

Deborah Parry's treatment is reported to be just as cruel. From the time the two nurses were arrested, they were unable to see each other. Separating witnesses, or alleged codefendants in this case, is a common police practice. The idea is to pit one against the other, or to prevent a collusion of events. It also allows the police the opportunity to apply a little trickery and deceit in gaining confessional justice.

As with Lucille McLauchlan, Deborah Parry was taken to an interrogation room. She too reports being the subject of insults, threats, physical abuse, and promises.

"Major Hamed has kept on coming in and out of the room and pulling my hair and slapping my face; still calling me a "son of a bitch." I was told to remove my abaya at this point and the police continually touched my breasts and private parts. One of the policemen whilst kneeling in front of me with his hands on my thighs and other policemen around me was licking his lips and asking me "Who initiated the sex with you and your girlfriend, Yvonne?" I kept on saying that I was not a lesbian and had boyfriends; they said "No, you son of a bitch, you are a killer and used to lick Yvonne until you killed her." All this time they were rubbing my thighs; I thought that I would be raped by them all; I was so, so frightened."

The police reportedly called Parry British trash, suggesting she killed another women at the hospital in 1994 while working under a different name. The police accused her of trying to kill other patients as well. Every time Parry attempted to deny the accusations, she was slapped in the face and called a "lesbian killer." It was as if the police would not accept any statement unless it was one they agreed with.

Some police often harbor a bias if not antipathy against homosexuality in general. Police officers, regardless of whether they are Saudi, Americans, or British, possess conservative outlooks, while pursuing a macho image; some hold sexist attitudes, and some may have morbid fascinations with lesbianism (as many men probably do but won't admit it).

Police officers are often under a great deal of pressure to solve crimes which are particularly gruesome. Additionally, police officers are generally intolerant of persons who challenge their authority or interfere with their quest for evidence.

The idea of intimate sexual activity between two women foster passions that translate into rage or jealously in some men. It is as if to ask what does she have that any other man or I do not have? It is a form of symbolic castration, a threat to masculinity. In addition, the Saudi's in general view homosexuality as abnormal, and Islam categorically opposes homosexuality.

As with McLauchlan, Parry also stated that she was denied water or use of a toilet. The police withheld any request until she confessed to the killing. Parry kept telling the police she did not kill Gilford.

"I said I did not kill her, she is a friend and I had not been to her room for 5-6 weeks as she had a friend and they like to cycle and swim and I was with a different group of friends in the desert on most of my days off."

It was becoming quite evident that whatever Parry said, the police would not believe her. Parry told the police she believed security guards were responsible for the murder, but such information failed to impress the police. She was the primary suspect and that was that. In a nearby room, Parry heard policemen shouting and a woman crying. She later realized that the other woman was McLauchlan.

During the intense questioning, Parry reported that she continually asked for legal advice from the British Embassy. She was told that the police in Saudi Arabia are the law and that the British are trash and Islam rules.

"When I was eventually allowed to use a toilet, I had to leave the door open and a man standing and watching me as I pass urine. I have never felt so frightened, scared and intimidated until that day. I was not treated like a human being. Even to pass feces I was watched."

Male officers continually monitored Deborah Parry. Like McLauchlan, she was fearful of rape and torture.

"Several times a policeman held a cigarette close to my eyes and I could feel the heat, it was unbearable."

The police allegedly made promises. The main promise, as mentioned several times during the interrogation, was that if she cooperated, she would be sent home in two weeks. Cooperation of course meant a full confession.

"I was promised and promised that if I cooperated I would be sent home in two weeks as it was only a small problem. The reason that they stated this they said was because we were Christians and so was Yvonne

and only Muslims were important in Saudi Arabia."

The police commanded Parry to remove her clothes. They took pubic hair samples with the hope of finding similar hairs on the body of Yvonne Gilford. If found, this would definitely add strength to the lesbian relationship theory.

"I am told to remove my clothes or they would do it for me. I removed them myself and they all surrounded me...one knelt down with his head just between my knees and removed some pubic hair with scissors...I think I was left undressed for approximately one hour but I am not sure...during this time my breasts were poked, fondled and pulled which caused great pain and touched my private parts."

The police threats intensified. Parry was told that unless she cooperated, the treatment would get worse. She finally reached the breaking point. *"I cannot take any more so I agree to write whatever the police wanted me to even though it was all lies."*

How long can a person deprived of sleep, food, and exposed to abuse and threats endure? Is it reasonable to assume anyone under such pressure would confess just to end the pain?

During the Vietnam War, American prisoners of war were psychologically and physically tortured to get them to confess to American aggression. They were deprived of sleep, bombarded with broken promises, and beaten. To the Vietnamese captors, a confession was crucial, in spite of the evidence against them (or lack thereof). It didn't matter how the confession was obtained. The ends justified the means. The confession was proof; it was crucial.

The first written statement made by Lucille McLauchlan was on December 19, the day of her arrest. Deborah Parry also made a number of written statements with the final one prepared on 23 December, 1996. Throughout the 10-day ordeal of questioning and abuse, the police kept telling the nurses to write drafts of their confessions.

The nurses were told that they would be kept in the police station until they made written statements that were acceptable to the police, and if they didn't they would be placed in a men's prison. On Monday, December 23, 1996, the nurses were placed into a room and told to make sure their written statements were the same.

Prior to writing their confessions, McLauchlan was told by the police she would be taken to see Parry. The police tell her that they will ask questions in Parry's presence about the death of Yvonne Gilford. According to McLauchlan, Officer Hamed wanted her to state in front of Parry that she saw Parry stab Yvonne Gilford, and also that McLauchlan knew that Parry and Gilford were lesbians.

McLauchlan was warned that if she said anything else to Parry, or refused to implicate Parry in the murder, *"two of the policemen will hold her down while the other one fucks her and they will all fuck her while the rest watch."*

The following are the translated confessions of Lucille McLauchlan and Deborah Parry given to the Saudi police several days before the handwritten confession. It is reported that several confessions were given to the police just after their arrest, although information about this is unclear.

TRANSLATION FOR LUCILLE MCLAUCHLAN

I, Lucille McLauchlan, of British nationality, 31 years of age, holding passport No. D12659214 issued in Glasgow on 23/3/1994, a Christian, a sister at King Fahd Military Hospital of Dhahran, being fully competent hereby confess voluntarily as follows:

On Wednesday 1/8/1417Ah corresponding to 11 December 1996, at 1:00 o'clock after midnight, and while I was in my room, I received a telephone call from the deceased, Yvonne Gilford of Australian nationality, who lived in apartment No. 3A, building No. 44, King Fahd Military Hospital of Dhahran, who asked me to visit her in her apartment and informed me that the Deborah Parry "Dibi," of British nationality was also there. It appeared to me that she was confused, and I told her that it was already late in the night. However, I noticed that she was irritated and, because of that, I left my building and went to her apartment in the neighboring building. I knocked at her door and she opened the door for me. Dibi was there and they were discussing their lesbian relationship which was not as active as it had been. She told me that Dibi refused to leave Yvonne's apartment. They asked me to intervene and assist them in solving the problem. We sat and talked about the problem until it was 4:45 am when both of them got upset.

Consequently, Dibi took a metal kettle which was there on the kitchen table. There was no water in that kettle. She threw the kettle at Yvonne. The kettle fell at Yvonne's face. Yvonne was hurt and fell down. Dibi kicked her on the face. While the victim was lying on the ground. Dibi once again entered the kitchen and fetched a kitchen knife of the type used for slicing bread. Meanwhile, Yvonne stood up and Dibi stabbed her on the chest whereupon Yvonne fell again on to the ground. Thereafter, Dibi sat on her and stabbed her several times on her neck and back; (before that and when they started to quarrel and before Yvonne was hit by the kettle, Yvonne pushed Dibi who fell on a green small table and consequently got hurt). Thereafter, Dibi took hold of a pillow which was lying at a short distance on the ground and put that pillow on Yvonne's face in order to prevent her from crying and that had caused her death. I have witnessed that event without doing anything. Thereafter, Dibi left the victim's body. I was terrified from what I saw and told Dibi that if Yvonne was able to talk to anybody we would be discovered. Dibi was relatively less irritated than me and said:

"Now we have to clean the place".

She entered the kitchen and started washing the same knife which she used in the stabbing. Thereafter, she dried that knife and placed it either in a drawer in the kitchen or on the kitchen table. Then she entered the bathroom, collected a white towel and cleaned the knife and the metal kettle, which I placed on the cooker after I had tried to fix its broken arm.

Then I took a wet piece of cloth, which was lying on the washing machine, and cleaned the blood on my left hand. Then, I threw that piece of cloth which fell near Yvonne's body. Thereafter, I and Dibi went to my flat and cleaned the traces of blood which appeared on our clothes. I remained in my flat and Dibi went to her flat and each of us took a bath and washed our clothes in order to remove any traces of blood.

Two days later, Dibi informed me that she had in her possession Yvonne's automatic teller machine card and she knew the secret number assigned for that card. Dibi did not tell me how she came to know that secret number. She suggested to me to go and withdraw money from Yvonne's account. I told her that the police might discover us. She said that was impossible. We actually went on three consecutive days and withdrew on each time SR5,000. The first time and the second time, it was me who withdrew the money. Dibi withdrew on the third time. On the fourth time which was the last, I withdrew SR5,000, whereupon I was caught by the police while I was there in the bank. I had in my possession Yvonne's automatic teller machine card. Dibi informed me of the secret number of that card which is 4663. I remitted some of the amounts which we have obtained to my account in Britain and I sent part of it by mail to my mother in Britain.

The reason for committing the crime is that Dibi loved Yvonne and did not want anybody else to share her that love. I have not reported the crime because I was terrified, and I hereby sign this confession.

Signed by Lucille McLauchlan

Now we consider the translated confession of Deborah Parry.

TRANSLATION FOR DEBORAH KIM PARRY

I the undersigned Deborah Kim Parry, of British nationality, passport No. 008132594, issued from U.K. on 25/2/1993, Residence Permit (Iqamah) No. 2122708221 issued from Al-Khobar Passport Authority on 19/4/14__, with my full capacity and without duress from anybody, I hereby admit and confess that in the night of 1-2/8/1417, corresponding to 11-12/12/1996, at 2:00 a.m., Yvonne telephoned Lucille McLauchlan and requested her to come to a room. I was with her at that time. Yvonne

requested me to have lesbian relationship with her. I refused her request.
When Lucille came to us I was crying because of the request of Yvonne to
have lesbian relationship with me. As a result of my refusal Yvonne was
nervous. Lucille tried to cool down the situation. But Yvonne also request-
ed Lucille to have lesbian relationship with her. Lucille also refused her
proposal. Lucille slapped Yvonne on her face. Yvonne fell on a small green
table which was in the room and as a result thereof the table was broken.
Yvonne got up and pushed me away and as a result thereof my back col-
lided against the chair. This was .... Meanwhile, all of us
were shouting. I took a metal jug from the table and threw it towards
Yvonne. The jug hit the left side of her head. Yvonne fell as a result of the
hit. She got up and went to the kitchen and brought a knife (the bread
knife) from the drawer of the kitchen. A fight took place. Yvonne was bru-
tally excited and she was trying to stab us with the knife.

I pushed her towards the bed she fell on the bed. When she fell on
the bed she was injured by the knife. She got up again and tried to stab
us by the knife. Again she fell and injured herself by the knife in her
thigh. Lucille and myself tried to push Yvonne towards the bed. At that
time I was slightly injured in my left hand by the knife which was in
the hand of Yvonne. Also Lucille was injured in her right thigh by the
knife which was in the hand of Yvonne. When we pushed her again
towards the bed the knife fell from her hand. Lucille took the knife and
stabbed Yvonne on her back. Also I took the knife and stabbed Yvonne.
I cannot remember the number of stabs. This happened within a short
time. We were very confused and scared. All this happened while we
were trying to defend ourselves from Yvonne. As a result of the fighting
and hitting there was blood on the ground and the bed. Some of the
flowers fell on the ground. We requested Yvonne to stop her acts. Time
was late when she died. I tired to make sure that she was still alive. So,
in order to check the pulse of her heart I put my finger on her neck.
There was no pulse. Lucille and myself laid her on the ground in order
to help her but we could not do anything because she was already
dead. While we were cleaning the room and the bed, a small pillow fell
on the face of Yvonne. We did not use that pillow to smother her. After
that I picked up the knife and washed the blood. Lucille dried the knife
with a piece of cloth. Lucille put the knife in the drawer of the kitchen.
The knife was of a brown handle. We placed the flowers back on the TV.
Using the kitchen washer we washed the blood off our hands. We dried
our hands using the same piece of cloth. We arranged the bed. We
quickly departed to my room. We, Lucille and myself sat together speak-
ing for approximately one hour in my room, say up to 3:00 or 3:30
a.m. I prepared myself to go to work in the morning. Lucille was free
and therefore she washed my clothes and her clothes. During the event,

she was dressed in the following: Grey trouser, white shirt and white sport shoes. I was dressed in the following: Black jeans trousers and purple tee shirt. My clothes that have been washed are now in my room. The motive behind the quarrel and fighting caused the death of Yvonne was her request to have lesbian relationship with me and Lucille. I no nothing about the banking card of the deceased. What I know is that you told me that you have found the card with Lucille using the same in one of bank's teller in Al-Khobar. We went together to Al-Khobar and I departed her when we left the taxi in front of the northern side of Al-Shola markets. Lucille went to the bank and I entered to the market to make shipping. I confess that the cause of the death of Yvonne Gilford, of Australian nationality, was what I explained above. Before going out of room I was certain that she was dead. Except the deceased, Lucille and myself there was no body else inside the room during the event. According I sign.

The undersigned, Deborah Kim Parry

Handwritten confessions were provided on December 23, 1996. We begin with McLauchlan's confession followed by Deborah Parry's confession. The handwritten confessions are presented as they actually appeared, complete with spelling and grammar errors.

Lucille McLauchlan handwritten confession:

My name is Lucille McLauchlan. This is my true statement of events, which took place on Thursday 11th December 1996. I would like to firstly like to state my first statement was incorrect and incomplete.

At 0100 hrs. on Thursday 12th December 1996 I received a telephone call from Yvonne Ruth Gilford asking me to come down to her apartment which was in building 44. She stated Deborah Parry was in her apartment and that Debbie was refusing to leave. Yvonne sounded agitated so I agreed to go to her apartment. On arriving at her apartment I found Deborah Parry and Yvonne inside. Yvonne opened the door to let me inside. The atmosphere was tense and Yvonne appeared frightened. Yvonne asked me to try and get Deborah to leave. I asked both of them what was wrong and Yvonne stated that she wanted to end her relationship with Deborah, but Deborah wanted the relationship to continue. The relationship between them was a sexual one and had been continuing since not long after Deborah's arrival in Saudi Arabia. Yvonne had told me of the relationship not long after it began. At no time did Yvonne approach me in this manner (sexual). She knew I had a boyfriend in Scotland and was to married in June 1997. My relationship with Yvonne was more like Mother/Daughter. In Yvonne's apartment I tried to talk to

Debbie and Yvonne and see if there was anything I could do to help. The three of us talked until about 0430. Yvonne at this time very frankly told Debbie that the relationship was over and that she wanted her to leave her apartment and not come back. At this point Debbie went berserk. Also I must state at this point that Debbie had been since I arrived in Yvonne's apartment acting strange. I mean by this she appeared to be on some kind of medication. I do not know if this is true or not. Debbie went into Yvonne's kitchen and picked up the kettle, which was sitting on the stove and threw it at Yvonne. It hit Yvonne on the forehead. Yvonne fell to the ground at this point. I picked her up and she seemed dazed. I slapped her twice on the face to see if she was conscious which she appeared to be at this time. I was screaming to Debbie that I would call security if she did not leave the apartment now. She unplugged the telephone went in to the kitchen and took a bread knife out of Yvonne's drawer. She came towards Yvonne and stabbed her under her breast. I think it was her left breast. Yvonne fell to the ground. Her face as on the left side of her body was positioned stomach down. Debbie sat on top of her and I seen her stab Yvonne in the neck and in her upper back. I think it was on the right side of her back. I had sunk into the hallway at this point screaming at her to stop. I was very frightened at this point and I was panicking. I cannot say definitely how many times Yvonne was stabbed. Debbie stood up and I approached Yvonne's body. She was still making noises from her mouth. I placed a pillow over her face to stop her making a noise. If security had come at this point to Yvonne's apartment I honestly believed they would think that I had stabbed Yvonne. I held the pillow over Yvonne's face until she stopped making a noise. I would like to state at this point that the pillow was actually a cushion. A square floral or pink one. At this point I remember saying to Debbie that we would be caught. I was sure someone must have heard all the shouting and screaming. Debbie was very calm at this point. She said "We'll clean up and everything would be ok." I agreed to this. I picked up the kettle and the handle of the kettle which was broken and gave it to Debbie. She went into the bathroom and got a white bath towel and firstly put the knife under the tap water over the kitchen sink. She cleaned the knife then dried it with the white towel. She then cleaned the kettle. I picked up a small green table which Debbie had broken when she had fallen on it previously. I put it in between Yvonne's table which had T.V. and video on it and her big dining table. I then picked up a wet waste to wash blood of my left wrist. I did this and dropped the wet waste on the floor either beside or on top of Yvonne's body. I was still stating to Debbie at this point we would be caught but she was very calm. The white towel she had in her hands was covered in blood. I think the towel was also dropped either beside or on top of Yvonne's body. Debbie and myself then took Yvonne's wallet which was sitting on top of her cabinet in between the living area and the hallway and removed her bankcard. Her PIN number was also in her wallet. Why she kept it in her wallet beside her card I do not know. We mentioned her PIN number which was 4663 with the intention of removing money from Yvonne's bank account. Both Debbie and myself then left Yvonne's apartment. We both went to my apartment. Debbie only stayed for about 1-2 minutes. She then left to go to her own apartment. It was approximately 5:10 am by this point. I must state that we left Yvonne's apartment at 5:00-5:10 am. There may be 5 minutes discrepancy in this. I took off my pajamas and my abaya and put it in the washing machine. I went to my apartment and had a shower. I put my t-shirt and my sweat pants on. I then made coffee and just sat in my room. I was still convinced at this point that either someone heard all the noise in Yvonne's room or had seen both Debbie and myself leaving Yvonne's apartment. I think Debbie stabbed Yvonne 3 or 4 times. This is what I actually saw myself, but I did cover my face with my hands so it may have been more than 3 or 4. The knife was a bread knife. The handle was brown approx. 5 cm long. The blade was silver in colour and about 20 cm long. It was approx. 3 cm wide from the handle but narrowed to the tip to a point. Just before the actual throwing of the kettle took place Debbie was being aggressive to Yvonne. Yvonne pushed Debbie backwards. Debbie fell onto her bottom on top of a small green table. The table was broken by Debbie falling on top of it. I had blood on my left wrist. I think I got this as I put the cushion over Yvonne's face. It may have been then or when I lifted Yvonne up off the floor after Debbie hit her with the kettle as Yvonne as bleeding at this point. I think I may also have gotten blood on my pajama bottoms and the bottom of my abaya. Again I do not know how much as I removed them as soon as I got back to my apartment and put them in the washing machine. On Monday the 16th December both Debbie and myself planned to use Yvonne's bankcard. Debbie was working night shift on this night so we agreed I would use the card. I must state at this point we did not know how much money was in the bank account. I Lucille McLauchlan used the card on Monday 16th December at Al-Ragi bank beside Al-Shulan Mall and withdrew SR 5000. On Tuesday 17th December both Debbie and myself went to Al-Rasheed Mall and withdrew SR 5000. The time was about 6:30 pm. On Monday 16th December the time was about 5 pm on Wednesday 18th December both Debbie and myself went to Saudi Houand bank and withdrew SR 5000. It was about 9 am. On these three occasions I actually used the bankcard. The amount was SR 5000. I got SR 8000 and Debbie SR 7000. On Thursday 19th December both Debbie and myself went to Arab National bank. The time as approx. 0845. Debbie went to Al Shula Mall while I went inside bank to use ATM. I withdrew SR 5000. It was at this point the police caught me. The first stab-Yvonne was standing facing

Debbie as she came out of the kitchen. Debbie came towards Yvonne and stabbed her under her left breast. Yvonne fell to the ground. Debbie sat on top of Yvonne and stabbed her in the neck then on her right upper back. This is the stabs I actually saw. After Yvonne was dead Debbie and myself cleaned the bread knife used to kill Yvonne. Debbie did this and dried it with a white towel. The kettle was wiped with the white towel. I picked up the broken green table and put it between the two tables in Yvonne's room. I cannot remember cleaning any other area of Yvonne's apartment.

Lucille McLauchlan

I Lucille McLauchlan would like to state that I was a partner by suffocating her with the pillow on the morning of December 12th 1996 which caused Yvonne's death I am truly sorry for my actions and the part I played in this murder I sign for what I have just written.

Lucille McLauchlan

Deborah Kim Parry's handwritten confession:

This is the true, full statement of myself Deborah Kim Parry, British national age 38 years of age, born 25th October, 1958. The statement is of the incident that took place on the 12th December, 1996, Thursday, at King Fahd Military Medical complex, Dhahran in Building 44. I live in Building 41 as does Lucille McLauchlan. Yvonne Gilford, Australian National, lived in Building 44. Following day duty in the renal transplant unit where I had worked for three weeks following transfer from male specialty one, I went to Yvonne's apartment as I had been having a lesbian relationship with her since not long after arriving at the hospital and saw her every day. We talked and watched television for a while until I went to my room to change into my black jeans and pink t-shirt. I washed my hair and fed the cat. When I went back to Yvonne Gilford's room she told me that Lucille McLauchlan had visited earlier. Yvonne and I sat and talked again until she told me that she wanted to end our relationship, as she had found someone else. I was upset and cried for a long time. Eventually Yvonne rang Lucille McLauchlan in her room as she did not know what to do. Yvonne let Lucy in the door of her apartment, this was at 1 am in the morning. We talked for a long time amongst ourselves, and then the argument became out of control. Yvonne Gilford became aggressive and Lucille it her in the face. I was pushed over a small table by Yvonne Gilford, I bruised my buttocks. I then stood up and took a kettle from the stove and threw it. It broke, as it had it Yvonne on the head, she was dazed, but very angry, as was everyone. I took a bread knife from the kitchen draw. It had a serrated edge and stabbed Yvonne, as to what I thought was only three times, I was not aware of anymore. They were to her chest, neck and back. Lucille and I were panic stricken at this stage, as Yvonne was hurt, but still alive. Lucille McLauchlan took a pink floral cushion and pressed it onto Yvonne Gilford's face until she stopped breathing. She was lying half on her back and half on her side at this stage. We were surprised that security had not heard any noise from inside of Yvonne's apartment at this time as it is very quiet on the compound in the early hours of the morning. It must have been approximately 0400 hrs in the morning by this time. I was surprised to have hardly any blood on my clothes. I had a cut on my left hand at this point, which Dr. Daoud later commented on at work. In the apartment the knife was washed and returned to the draw, it was dried on a white towel from the bathroom by one of us. I was not sure if Lucille had also been involved in a lesbian relationship with Yvonne Gilford of Building 44. Although she had a boyfriend in England, but that does not mean anything. The broken kettle was wiped also using the white bathroom towel. It may have been a hospital towel and returned to the bathroom. The small table was picked up by Lucille after she had suffocated Yvonne with the cushion, either pink or floral. I returned the silk flowers to the television set, which was on the video that Yvonne had recently bought. The coffee cups, teacups and cutlery that we had used that evening were washed by us and placed in the appropriate cupboards and draws. We left Yvonne Gilford's room. That is myself and Lucille McLauchlan at around about 0500 hours in the morning. We both had abayas on at this time, it was cool outside and we often wore abayas on the compound. Before leaving the room the telephone was disconnected from the wall and Lucille McLauchlan took Yvonne Gilford's bankcard and personal number (PIN number) from her wallet which was on a cabinet between the lounge and kitchen, it was a wooden cabinet. Lucille looked through the peep-hole in the door at this time to make sure that no one was around. We were very, very frightened at this point as it was all an accident. We momentarily spoke in Lucille McLauchlan's room until approximately ten past five in the morning. We discussed the awful accident. I returned to my room as I was on duty at 0700 hrs in the morning, and had to wash my clothes and have shower and hair wash before leaving. The next few evenings were either spent talking to Lucille McLauchlan or on night duty. My cut on my left had was very painful and my left buttock was bruised on the evening of the 16th of December, 1996. Lucille McLauchlan had gone into the bank in Khobar and drawn out money. She gave some to me. We both went to Al Rhasheed shopping mall on the evening of the 17th December, 1996. I think it was and drew more out. This was a Tuesday evening. We shopped and ate there. I bought sewing materials and a new watch as did Lucille McLauchlan. I also bought two new rings and a new red and white nightshirt. I collected photographs for one of my friend's here. Caroline left us when we went to the bank machine. We went home by limousine. We then

*again went to Khobar, Shola Mall on the morning of the 19th December
1996, which was a Thursday and once again drew out money from the
machine. I bought items for my cat in the pet shop, in total Lucille had
eight thousand Saudi Riyals and I had seven thousand Saudi Riyals. I
bought several material items with this. I bought a new Continental quilt
set. One for my room and one for use if I went to the people that I am
friendly with. I bought many small things, such as a rug for my room and
some new French underwear that I bought at Al Rhasheed mall. The most
money went on the underwear as this cost six hundred and ninety Saudi
Riyals and a gold chain and palm tree which I bought also at Al Sholla
shopping mall on the first occasion.*

*I do not know what Lucille McLauchlan did with her money. On one
occasion I changed my own salary at the bank with Caroline and Lucille
having had coffee at the Vienna Coffee Shop in Khobar. I telexed approximately two thousand Saudi Riyals to the National Westminster Bank in
Alton in Hampshire, England. I have the rest of my salary in my handbag
at the police station. On several of these occasions Lucille McLauchlan and
I parted to do our own shopping. On the morning of the 20th December,
1996. Lucille McLauchlan went to the bank machine and I went into Al
Shola shopping mall. This is where I was arrested in the north part of the
mall. And escorted to the police station in Dharran by an un-uniformed
police man. Since then I have spent the days at the police station and in
prison and have only received one hundred and fifty Riyals from my
handbag which is at the police station. The whole incident was an accident in Building 44 at the King Fahd medical center complex hospital.
Dharan, Kingdom of Saudi Arabia*
    Deborah Kim Parry

There are differences in the confessions. While both nurses agree that
a lesbian relationship was attempted or alleged between Gilford and
Parry, they differ on who initiated the encounter. In Parry's handwritten
confession, she confesses to having a lesbian relationship with Yvonne
Gilford. However, in the translated confession Parry states that it was
Gilford who attempted having a lesbian relationship with Parry. The
events that took place after McLauchlan's arrival at Gilford's apartment
that morning also differ. In Parry's translated confession, she directly
names McLauchlan as a major player in the killing of Yvonne Gilford.

Both confessions are the only hard evidence, offered by the police,
against the nurses. By examining the confessions, one is left with the
impression that they were given under duress. But there are inconsistencies in the statements given both in the handwritten statements and translations. Let's look at some of those inconsistencies.

Beginning with the nurses' handwritten statements, both agree there is a conflict between Yvonne Gilford and Debbie Parry over a sexual relationship. But as to who initiated it or who was involved becomes another matter. Both nurses agree that before the killing, they were together in Yvonne Gilford's apartment. As to the reasons they were there, McLauchlan states that Gilford wanted to end a relationship with Parry, but Parry wanted it to continue and "went berserk," attacking Gilford.

McLauchlan appears to offer herself as a go between with Gilford and Parry, trying to be a mediator for the two lovers. McLauchlan pins Parry as the one who took a kitchen knife out of the drawer to stab Gilford several times. McLauchlan admits placing a pillow over Gilford's face to stop her from screaming. McLauchlan also admits taking Gilford's bankcard and PIN number.

As to Debbie Parry's handwritten statement, she admits having a lesbian relationship with Gilford, and as stated by McLauchlan, Gilford wanted to terminate the relationship. That much the nurses agree on. However, the events that transpired afterward differ. Parry states that Gilford was the one who became aggressive not her. After Gilford wanted to end the relationship, she attacked both McLauchlan and Parry.

Parry admits throwing a metal teapot at Gilford, hitting her in the head. Parry then took a knife from Gilford's drawer, stabbing her several times. Their statements are consistent on McLauchlan placing the pillow over Gilford's mouth. Parry admits cutting her hand in the attack, and McLauchlan taking Gilford's bankcard and PIN number. Both statements concur on cleaning the apartment after the attack, an attempt to conceal the crime.

Both nurses remember the details of the murder and their actions afterward. This leads one to believe that the confessions were dictated or they were at the death scene. But now we turn to the translations of the nurses' confessions, which differ significantly, from the handwritten versions. The translated versions of both nurses were reportedly taken a few days before the handwritten confessions.

In the translated version of Debbie Parry's confession, she offers a different story. She states she didn't have a lesbian relationship with Yvonne Gilford, as requested by Gilford. On the evening before the murder, while at Gilford's apartment, the two were discussing Gilford's sexual needs. McLauchlan was called to the apartment to help intervene, since Gilford was becoming very upset at Parry's refusal to participate in a lesbian relationship. Parry then states that Gilford asked McLauchlan to have a relationship, with McLauchlan refusing as well. According to Parry, this angered McLauchlan who slapped Gilford in the face, causing her to fall on a small green table. Parry blames McLauchlan for stabbing Gilford, and denies taking the bankcard from Gilford's purse.

McLauchlan's translated confession is even more inconsistent. McLauchlan states that she was called to Gilford's apartment to intervene in a dispute between the two. This is similar to her handwritten statement, that Parry and Gilford were involved as lesbians. McLauchlan blames Parry for throwing the metal jug at Gilford, stabbing and suffocating Gilford with the pillow. McLauchlan did not admit taking a bankcard, but writes that two days later Parry informs her that she took Gilford's bankcard. McLauchlan admits going to the bank with Parry to withdraw money from Gilford's account.

So what do we make of these confessions? Whom do we believe? Are both the handwritten and translated versions total fabrications? Remember that the translated versions were taken a few days before the handwritten ones were given. Does this inconsistency suggest a problem in credibility, an indication of guilt? Was there a problem in translation, intentional or otherwise? We are dealing with a nurse who is a convicted thief, and another suffering from severe emotional stress.

Again, the primary evidence against the nurses is their confessions, which is the only real evidence against them, and all that is really required under Saudi law. Of course, we will learn later that the nurses subsequently withdrew their confessions. Who are the liars in this tale? Whom do we believe? For the record, a forensic psychology expert, Professor David Cooke of Glasgow Caledonian University, reviewed the written confessions. In his report, he believed the confessions should be regarded as untrustworthy and totally unreliable.

On Christmas Day, 1996, both nurses were taken to Gilford's apartment, where the police took a video of the nurses reenacting the crime. The nurses were told what to do and how to reenact the crime. The police tell the nurses that the video was needed to finish their report; if they fail to cooperate, they will not be allowed to return home. Once again, the nurses allege that threats are directed toward them.

After the ten days of brutal questioning, the nurses confess to the murder of Yvonne Gilford. According to the Dhahran Police report (No. 21/13/2/882/S, dated 25/December/1996), the fruits of the police interrogation are summarized:

"After investigation and questioning of the two accused, Lucille McLauchlan informed the investigator that on Wednesday evening /Thursday morning, at 1:00 A.M. she received a telephone call from Yvonne Roseanne Gilford telling her that Deborah Kim Parry was in her room and refused to leave and she asked her to come to her room to assist in convincing Deborah Kim Parry to leave and she wen immediately and she tried to solve the problem. She said that there was a sexual relationship between Yvonne and Deborah and that Yvonne wanted to terminate that relationship, while Deborah objected. She further added that the dis-

cussion continued until 4:00 A.M., when both Yvonne and Deborah became upset and thereupon Deborah threw a kettle at Yvonne's face, pursuant to which Yvonne fell on the ground. Lucille added that she tried to help Yvonne to stand up and she slapped her on the face twice. She went on to say that Deborah entered the kitchen, fetched a knife and stabbed Yvonne several times and she remembers that these stabs were just below Yvonne's left breast she believes. She added that Yvonne fell down and Deborah continued to stab her on the neck and the upper part of her back. She further added that Yvonne was making a noise from her mouth, whereupon Lucille placed a pillow upon her face in order to prevent her from making a noise, until she died. Lucille told the investigator that after they were sure Yvonne was dead, Lucille and Deborah cleaned the place, rearranged the room and wipe away any traces adding that Deborah was injured at the lower part of her back when she was pushed by Yvonne. She also added they stole Yvonne's cash card and left the room around 5:00 A.M. Deborah Kim Parry was also interrogated and her statements were identical to those of Lucille. Deborah mentioned that she could not remember some of the stabs because she did not know what she was doing. Their confessions were legally endorsed."

Up to this point there had been many verbal whacks at the Saudi police, especially the officer who conducted the interrogations. The nurses accused the police of physical abuse, threats of rape or torture, and sexual harassment. But what do the police say? In a rare interview with a Scottish newspaper, Saudi police chief Colonel Hamad Al-Omari, who was the main villain accused of using physical force and sexual abuse to force the nurses to confess, rejected the allegations. "I never put a hand on them and I am positive not one finger was laid on them by my officers. They claim we tortured them or tried to rape them, but we were never alone with them, never at all."

Does the alleged mistreatment of Parry and McLauchlan by the Saudi police come as a surprise? In a system where women for the most part are viewed as second-class citizens, the treatment may not be surprising. On the other hand, why would the police risk an international incident by mistreating two expatriates? Why would the police create a situation calling into question their competence and unwelcome scrutiny? Perhaps these questions will never be fully answered.

McLauchlan describes life in the Saudi jail as hell. The tension between her and Parry was getting worse. Many women in the jail were imprisoned for drug offenses, or sex-related crimes such as having children without husbands. Women are allowed to keep their children while serving their time. McLauchlan offers evidence of her early experiences in jail, and tensions with Parry:

"The noise is unbelievable. Babies crying, people talking and arguing.

All the different languages. Christ, am I really here? Debbie starts blab-
bering as soon as she opens her eyes. I think she's had some kind of break-
down. I really do. I've never seen anyone like her before. She's freaking
out, shaking, talking really fast. Her look frenzied. She's really losing it.
Abby looks at her in disbelief. Deb just keeps on saying 'What a night-
mare.' She doesn't have to bloody tell me that."

On December 28, 1996, the nurses were told to clean up. They had
been imprisoned for ten days without the benefit of legal counsel, family contacts, or embassy assistance. However, this day was different.
For the first time since their arrest at the shopping mall on December
19, they finally were permitted to meet Tim Lamb of the British
Embassy.

Surprisingly, Major Hamed (later promoted to Colonel), the chief
interrogator and nemesis of the nurses, was also present. The nurses
found this odd, because Hamed had told the nurses a few days before
that since he had their confessions, his investigation was finished, and the
nurses would no longer see him. They were told the game was over and
they would return home soon.

The meeting with Lamb was not encouraging. He advised the nurses
that they were in "big trouble" and would not be allowed to leave soon.
Of course, this was contrary to what Major Hamed had promised all
along: "Confess and it will be all over" was what the nurses were told
over and over. The nurses' gullibility and trust had backfired, just as the
young simple-minded virgin is seduced and betrayed by a fast-talking
lover.

Feeling betrayed by Major Hamed, and mustering courage in the
presence of a British official, the bottled-up frustrations and fears experienced by the nurses over the past ten days exploded. The nurses let it
out, telling Lamb of their physical abuse over the past ten days, insisting
their confessions were the product of duress. They wanted to retract their
bogus confessions.

Lamb assured the nurses a doctor would see them, and that he would
look into the case. On December 29, at the request of the embassy, the
nurses were taken to the hospital where three doctors examined them;
however, no physical evidence of abuse was found on the women: no
marks, bruises, or tissue damage.

Deborah Parry and Lucille McLauchlan were not the first Westerners
allegedly forced into confessions. As reported in the *Los Angeles Times* in
1997, 10 years ago, Monica Hall, an "operating-room nurse from Dublin,
was accused of murdering her supervisor, Helen Feeney, at their hospital in Taif, Saudi Arabia." On July 12, 1986, Hall and her then-husband,
Peter, were accused of the crime.

"I was a woman alone, at the hands of ruthless experts," she recounts,

undergoing 11 days of intense questioning. Like the nurses, she, too, was deprived of sleep, given confusing information, interrogated at odd hours, and forced to reenact the crime.

"They kept telling me that Peter had confessed—why couldn't I? They kept insisting I was lying." Like McLauchlan and Parry, Hall finally broke down and signed a confession, believing that she was signing her death warrant.

"I was beyond caring," she says. *"Anything to stop the ruthless battery."*

In spite of all the controversy of forced confessions, a major question remains unanswered. What about the bankcard that McLauchlan allegedly had in her possession on the day of her arrest? The police also indicated they had a video of McLauchlan withdrawing funds from Gilford's bank account.

This fact was also reported in various media sources. However, no such video was ever produced at the lengthy court trial. Saudi banks are not equipped with such technology, a fact that the women's lawyers say proves that there never could have been any such evidence in the first place. Additionally, videotaping women is simply not done in the Kingdom.

Reports surfaced that on the day of the arrest, the bank manager, equipped with a tape recorder and under police instruction, questioned McLauchlan about the withdrawal, to which she responded she was making it on behalf of her colleague. However, the defense claims that those withdrawals were made after the arrests and interrogations. In other words, could the police and the bank manager have staged the withdrawals?

Reports circulated that McLauchlan telexed 3,003 pounds back to Britain immediately after Gilford's death. This exceeded her monthly salary of 980 pounds. The money was sent to her fiancé, now husband, Grant Ferrie. McLauchlan has always denied using the card, and claims it and the cash were planted on her during her interrogation.

Where did the pounds come from? McLauchlan reportedly kept a stash fund. She revealed that she brought over 2,000 pounds from Britain to Saudi Arabia for emergencies and sent it back because she feared it would be stolen. She kept some cash in her bedroom for emergencies. Of course if this were true, then why was she allegedly borrowing money?

The written confessions of both nurses and the video reenactment were necessary to convince the judge that they were indeed guilty. In fact, the only evidence disclosed by the police was copies of the written statements by the nurses while in police custody, and a copy of the autopsy report. Despite the fact that both women gave blood, skin and fingerprint samples to the investigators, no forensic evidence or other testimony was officially produced linking them to the killing.

One Saudi source close to the case said that there was no trace of blood on the knife allegedly used as the murder weapon. Forensic science, while used in the investigative process, is not considered important under Saudi law as long as there is a confession. Remember that under Islamic law, a confession is a cleansing or repentance, the first step in redemption.

No explanation was ever sought by the court as to why a cheap gold chain, belonging to none of the three women, was found at the scene; nor why a clump of blonde hair was found in the hand of Yvonne Gilford. Both of the accused are brunettes. In a letter sent to the judges of the Sharia Major court in Al-Khobar, as prepared by The International law firm of Osama Al-Solaim and Ghassan Al-Awaji (dated June 23, 1997), the theory of the crime and demands for punishment were officially presented. The Saudi lawyers, who were representing heirs of Yvonne Gilford, wrote the following:

"On December 12, 1996, at the apartment of Yvonne Gilford in the King Fahad Medical Complex, in Dhahran, Deborah Parry hit Yvonne with a metal kettle on her head and stabbed her three times with a sharp knife to different parts of her body. One of these stabs was underneath the left breast. The second and third stabs were to the neck and back of the deceased.

After the deceased had fallen down, Deborah Parry stabbed her several times to various parts of the body. Thereafter, Deborah Parry cleaned the knife and participated with her colleague, Lucille McLauchlan, in the theft of SR 15,000 from the deceased account by using the deceased ATM card, which they stole from the deceased. Deborah's share of the stolen amount was SR7,000.

Based on the above, we request that the accused be ordered to pay the amount of SR 7,000 representing her share of the stolen money. We also request that she be punished with Kisas (beheading).

Lucille McLauchlan, of the British nationality, has also participated with Deborah Parry in murdering Yvonne Gilford. After, Deborah Parry had stabbed the deceased as explained above, Lucille McLauchlan sat on the body of the deceased, and suffocated her by placing a cushion on her face while the deceased was bleeding.

As a nurse, Lucille McLauchlan could have provided first aid to the deceased, or could have carried her to the nearby hospital. However, Lucille McLauchlan intended not to help or assist the deceased. Furthermore, she joined Deborah Parry in cleaning the place where the crime occurred and in the theft of SR15,000 from the deceased's account. The share of Lucille McLauchlan's stolen money was SR8,000.

Based on the above, we request that Lucille McLauchlan be ordered to repay the said amount and be punished with kisas."

The police case against the nurses was based entirely on their confessions and evidence of the relationship between the nurses. Ghassan Al Awaji admitted the only real evidence against the nurses was their confessions.

The following evidence, mostly circumstantial, supports the police version of the case:

• They were friends and work associates of Gilford, therefore they had knowledge of her lifestyle.

• There were allegations that all three nurses were lesbians, and they had had disputes in the past.

• Lucille McLauchlan was one of the last people to see Gilford on the day she was murdered.

• McLauchlan used Gilford's bankcard after her death, and was reportedly caught by a bank manager using the card. There were a number of withdrawals from Gilford's account after her death, and McLauchlan made several money transfers back to the United Kingdom after Gilford's death..

• After intense police questioning, the nurses confessed to the crime. Why would they confess unless they were guilty?

• Gilford's apartment was remarkably clean for being the scene of a murder and there was no evidence of forced intrusion, suggesting that the crime had to be committed by someone close to Yvonne Gilford.

• McLauchlan's fingerprints were found in Gilford's apartment.

• McLauchlan was reportedly seen washing her clothes at an unusual hour after the murder of Gilford.

It is this circumstantial evidence that most probably led the police to believe that they had the right persons, and to zealously seek their confessions. They believed that such evidence would be enough to gain a confession from the two.

Without doubt, the nurses needed legal representation by attorneys who could construct a rigid defense and challenge the evidence. But the Sharia courts do not recognize criminal defense attorneys. Since the initial visit of Tom Lamb, efforts were underway to find a powerful, but knowledgeable attorney versed in the Islamic jurisprudence. Unknown to the nurses at the time, they were faced with the possibility of execution.

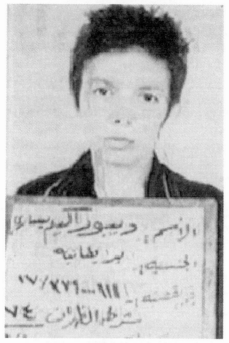

Police photo of Deborah Parry shortly after her arrest

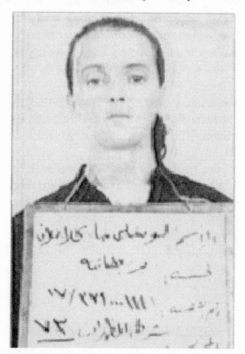

Police photo of Lucille McLauchlan shortly after her arrest

Yvonne Gilford in her apartment

Salah Al-Hejailan at work in his office

6
Defending Against Injustice

In sports competition, it is often said the offense wins games, but defense wins championships. The real test in sports competition is how well the defense holds up in the final minutes of a bitterly fought contest. Criminal defense is a serious undertaking, exploring all legal angles and theories. The first and foremost responsibility of a defense attorney is to defend clients, even if the evidence is overwhelming, and the accused may in fact be guilty.

In his book, *The Best Defense,* renowned American constitutional law attorney Alan M. Dershowitz offers the following principle: *"Almost all criminal defendants are in fact guilty, and everyone including the judge knows this."* To overcome this awesome challenge, lawyers must challenge evidence against their client(s) by showing it was the result of unlawful measures, or is insufficient to convict. The defense lawyer must be aggressive, persistent, and have a strong belief in the presumption of innocence. However, the opportunity for a criminal defense lawyer to flex his legal muscles in the courtroom does not happen in the Kingdom.

For a week after their arrest on December 19, 1996, the nurses were imprisoned in the women's section of the Dammen prison, denied permission to see anyone until their meeting with British Embassy representative Tom Lamb. Their fate appeared sealed, considering that the police pegged the nurses as murderers, in spite of the limited circumstantial evidence and retracted confessions.

During their interrogation, the nurses were shuttled back and forth between prison and the police station. They were initially denied access to an attorney and allegedly looked upon with utter scorn by the investigating officers. After their confessions, and despite their retractions, life in prison was agonizing hell. The nurses were taken to Damman central prison, and led into a cell with 10 Saudi women, described by witnesses as a stinking, cockroach-infested milieu, consisting of four hole-in-the-ground lavatories shared by 70 women.

In her book written after returning to the safety of the United Kingdom (which is discussed in more length in the next chapter), McLauchlan proclaims her innocence and describes the deplorable jail conditions where she was confined for 17 months:

The jail has seven cells with twelve beds in each. There are four toilets —holes in the ground. There are no showers, only taps beside the holes in the ground. The toilet area is disgusting. It's four cubicles with holes in the ground. There is a tap halfway up the wall. The tiles on the walls are covered in dirt, slime and shit. The doors are all rotting away. There are two big plastic bins beside the entrance leading to the toilets. No lids on them. They are full to the brim with disposable nappies and used sanitary towels. The smell is unbelievable. There are open drains dotted about the floor of the toilet area. The smell from them is the worst, and I know that open drains mean cockroaches. I am terrified of beasties of any sort. Jesus, I cannot believe I'm here. I'm not a bad person. I've never hurt anybody before. I'm no angel and have done a couple of things in my life I deeply, deeply regret, but I don't deserve what's happening to me.

Since their pre-trial incarceration, the nurses hadn't had much to do but lie around waiting for visits from their lawyers or family. For several weeks, McLauchlan and Parry were in the company of another nurse, an American charged with possessing cannabis (marijuana). They joked together about the cockroaches and horrible surroundings. To keep busy and their minds occupied, the nurses attended classes on Islam, a form of education and moral cleansing for prison inmates. It is not unusual for prisoners in some nations to be given political or religious education as part of their rehabilitation.

At night prisoners slept on steel beds covered by thin mattresses and by day were confined to their tiny cell. In the cell the constant foul odor of urine, sweat, and other undesirable bodily discharges filled the air. Both lost weight rapidly, suffered hair loss and severe dental problems.

Prisons are not structured for entertainment. Prisoners in the United States often spend waking hours watching television, playing dominoes, working on appeals, anything to pass time. Sexual deviance and violence are common reactions to overcome boredom in prison, or establish control over another weaker inmate. The prison experiences of the nurses were not sweet; nor would they be in England, the United States or other supposedly civilized countries.

Generally, Saudi prisons are not known to be dangerous or violent, and treatment for ordinary inmates is not particularly cruel. Yet, other than Islamic teachings, little attention is given to rehabilitation or training; a common complaint in Western prisons as well. As with most prisons anywhere, boredom is a particular problem. However, most Saudi prisoners are released for good behavior after serving three-quarters of their sentences. Medical care is provided, and female inmates are allowed to keep their young children in prison.

According to a United States Department of State human rights report (1997), Prison and jail conditions vary throughout the Kingdom. Prisons generally meet minimum international standards and provide air-conditioned cells, good nutrition, regular exercise, and careful patrolling by prison guards. However, some police station jails are overcrowded and unsanitary. Authorities generally allow family members visitation rights. In addition, and in the spirit of reform, King Fahd established boards of Investigation and Public Prosecution, organized on a regional basis. The members of these boards have the right to inspect prisons, review prisoners' files, and hear their complaints.

The Government does not permit human rights monitors to visit prisons or jails. However, diplomats, and in some cases, family, are granted access to incarcerated foreign citizens; The Government does not allow impartial observers of any type access to specialized Ministry of Interior prisons, where it detains persons accused of political subversion.

Amnesty International reports of prison conditions often remarkably differ from other points of view. The alleged torture and ill treatment of political prisoners and common-law criminals in police stations and prisons is routine in Saudi Arabia. Methods include electric shocks, beatings, falaqa (beating on the soles of the feet), and ta'liq (suspension by the wrist from the ceiling or a high window). Such practices are often used to extract "confessions," especially during pre-trial incommunicado detention. These punishments reportedly are reserved for political dissidents and Third World prisoners without political clout. However, the accuracy or extent of these claims remains an open topic since there is no official documentation.

But one fact is clear; the prison industry in Saudi Arabia is not a principal growth business as it is in the United States or other prison-happy nations. Therefore, it is no wonder complaints of human rights violations are reported because the Saudis are inexperienced in dealing with masses of incorrigibles. However, if the Amnesty reports are accurate, then their inexperience does not justify their brutal behavior.

Confinement in any system, for any reason, has a way of causing havoc to anyone's mental health. Such was the case for Deborah Parry. There were concerns about Parry's mental health, since she had a history of depression undoubtedly due to her string of family problems. Yet, she reportedly held up well despite the isolated conditions.

In a letter to a co-worker and friend, Parry described her prison experiences. Parry said she was doing well and made no complaints about being mistreated in prison. Prison conditions were tolerable, according to visits by family members, including Jon Ashbee, Parry's brother-in-law. Ashbee basically put his life on hold by making over a dozen trips to Saudi Arabia, a familiar passenger on British Air, to visit Parry in prison and to help win her release.

Yet the tension of constraint, uncertainty, and inactivity eventually began to take its toll. McLauchlan describes in her diary of January 24, 1997, how Deborah Parry's mental state began to deteriorate. She writes of Parry acting weird and seeing a prison psychiatrist. McLauchlan recounts her reasons for signing the confessions as well. Her reasons are because of her fear of being raped by the Saudi police.

As weeks passed, detention conditions improved. Visits from embassy officials increased, and the case was becoming big news in Australia, Great Britain, and the United States, where friends, associates, and legal scholars offered opinions on the case. Obviously the attention and scrutiny by the Western media had an indirect impact on their treatment in prison.

With two Western nurses jailed in a Muslim country, the case was developing political overtones. According to Britain's ambassador to Saudi Arabia, Andrew Green, both women were "bearing up quite well under the circumstances." It is rare for a British citizen to run afoul of the law in Saudi Arabia. Over 30,000 British citizens live and work in Saudi Arabia, and many have lived there for years. Only "a handful" ever got into trouble, and as of January, 1998, just five British citizens were jailed, including the two nurses.

On January 4, 1997, the nurses had their first meeting with defense attorneys. Contacted by the British Embassy in late December, 1996, one of the most prestigious and experienced law firms in the Kingdom, the firm of Salah Al-Hejailan, agreed to represent the nurses pro bono, a legalistic term meaning "representation at no charge."

The firm of Salah Al-Hejailan consists of 14 associates, some American and British, specializing in various areas of law. The firm, with offices worldwide, has an established legal reputation in International business. But why would Hejailan and his team of seasoned lawyers be interested in the case? Why would they defend without charging a fee? Hejailan didn't need the funds, so was he seeking publicity as some strongly suggest, or was it a challenge, an opportunity to test the criminal adversary process in a system with no such precedent?

The reason was simple: Hejailan was asked by the British embassy to represent the nurses. He had performed legal work in the past for the

British government and in an unprecedented case such as this, a reputable Saudi attorney was the perfect solution to what was becoming a highly scrutinized international fiasco. Hejailan's expertise was the logical choice. Was he seeking publicity in an attempt to inflate his ego? Maybe so or maybe not, but many lawyers are showman if not entertainers. As long as the job gets done and the client gets effective representation, who cares?

Known as a skillful, but often contentious litigator, Salah Al-Hejailan is the principal of the law firm of the same name, which he founded in 1968. Educated in the United States (University of Southern California) and Egypt, Hejailan is regarded as one of the pre-eminent commercial and litigation attorneys in the Middle East, and his firm is the largest commercial and litigation practice in Saudi Arabia. He has also served the government of Saudi Arabia in various capacities including that of Legal Adviser to the Council of Ministers, Kingdom of Saudi Arabia. There is another side to Hejailan as well. He is critical of the confessional-based system of Saudi justice.

In an interview with a British news magazine in 1997, Hejailan criticized the Saudi justice system and judges for failing to have lawyers around. However, the criticism is more of a frustration, rather than an indictment against the Sharia law.

Yet, the assault on the Saudi criminal justice process was a bold move by Hejailan. It was a rare attack on the conservative criminal court system by a member of the Saudi legal community. Criticism of the system becomes more meaningful when it comes from an insider rather than some detached Westerner. But insider criticism of the Saudi system is not new.

There have been complaints of government oppression, and the paternalistic way in which women are treated. Some of these criticisms have come from younger members of the royal family as well.

The Hejailan law firm was not alone in its quest to defend the nurses. Other attorneys joined the conflict on behalf of the nurses. To avoid confusion, let's review the major legal players representing the nurses. Rodger Pannone of the firm of Pannone and Partners, of Manchester, England, represented the family interests of Deborah Parry; Peter Watson of Levy and McRae of Glasgow, Scotland, represented the family legal interests of Lucille McLauchlan. (Another Scottish Solicitor from Dundee, W.G. Boyle, represented Lucille McLauchlan's interests after she returned to her native Scotland.)

In addition to Pannone, Watson, and the Hejailan team, other attorneys were brought on board. Since Yvonne Gilford had heirs in Australia, there was a need to have legal representation from her home country in the event information was required through the Australian courts. As we will see later, crucial facts were necessary from Australia regarding Gilford's heirs. Michael Burnett, of the law firm of Minter, Ellison, Bake, O'Loughlin, located in Adelaide, Australia assisted Hejailan in determining the mental state of Yvonne Gilford's mother, Muriel Gilford. So there was now legal representation from a fourth country, Australia.

Frank Gilford, the victim's brother, in his quest for justice needed lawyers as well. In addition to his Saudi team, John Keen and Michael Abbott represented Frank's legal interests especially during the sensitive and often tenuous blood money negotiation process.

One particular lawyer, Jim Phipps, representing Frank Gilford's interests, was a barrister Lucille McLauchlan particularly loathed. McLauchlan writes how Phipps attempted to represent her when she was first arrested. Having been informed Hejailan already represented her and Parry, he turned to the other side, switching from a potential advocate to predator. This suggests yet another unethical practice some lawyers undertake who are out to make a name or add to their bank account.

McLauchlan offers her insight into this sad event.

"I think I can be forgiven for being deeply cynical about the law, whatever form it takes. Later I was to find out that an American lawyer, Jim Phipps, who worked for a firm based in Salt Lake City, had approached the British Embassy in Riyadh on his own initiative and offered to represent us just as Salah was appointed. When he was told our defense was already taken care of, he contacted Frank Gilford and became his legal representative. At this stage, Gilford was still insisting his sister's murderers should be beheaded and Salah thought it was in our favour that Phipps was a Mormon and therefore a God-fearing man who would persuade Gilford to be more reasonable. Salah was wrong. Phipps, perhaps because he didn't get the 'juicier' job of defending me and Debs, seemed determined to do all he could to damn us."

On Sunday January 12, 1997, the two women saw their relatives for the first time since the dreadful saga began. The nurses were allowed to meet with their relatives for nearly two hours that day. Both women were described as *"doing well"* in spite of the restrictive conditions, and the monotony of confinement.

On January 13, 1997, a day after meeting with their relatives and nearly one month after the killing, Deborah Parry and Lucille McLauchlan appeared before a panel of three judges, their first court appearance since the arrest. The hearing was basically informal; the nurses were informed of their charges and reason for arrest. During the eventful hearing, the Saudi attorney representing the family of Yvonne Gilford demanded the death penalty for the two British colleagues. For the first time reality was closing in as it became clear the prosecution wanted their heads, literally.

"It was about midday when we were put in the back of the prison van and had leg shackles and handcuffs put on us. It was routine procedure for any prisoners being taken to court, though on subsequent visits the shackles were forgotten and only the handcuffs used. There was one female guard as an escort, and three men from the male section of the prison, one with a machine-gun slung over his shoulder. It was a 15-minute drive through the town to the court which was an undistinguished, white four-story building surrounded by similar office blocks. Inside, there were a lot of people in shackles, almost all men, moving awkwardly along the corridors or sitting on chairs outside rooms with guards standing over them. We had to hobble up the stairs to the courtroom on the first floor. It was undistinguished, a big room with two large ceiling fans lazily rotating to keep the air moving. Three judges in traditional thobes and red and white checked gutras sat at a long table covered with folders and pieces of paper and a court clerk sat off to one side. The various lawyers sat directly in front of the judges, with the Saudi prosecutors firm, then Mike Dark and Mutlaq-al-Mutlaq and another Saudi called Anwar, and then the American Jim Phipps and a couple of others representing Frank Gilford. Debbie and I sat at the side beside the door with the interpreter. The Charge d'Affaires from the British Embassy in Riyadh, William Patey, was there with us the first time, and Lawson Ross too, from the British Trade Office.

It was reassuring to have them there. They had been given special dispensation to attend because normally Saudi courts don't let anyone in who isn't directly connected with the case. The judges never looked at us once. Occasionally, I would almost make eye contact with one of them but then he would look away at the critical moment. It is a cultural thing with Saudis, I was told. Men and women don't look at each other if they can possibly avoid it. In fact, in the streets the Matowa have the right to inflict summary punishment on anybody whom they consider to be looking at a member of the opposite sex in an improper manner.

Jim Phipps, though, was a different proposition. He stared at us, looked us up and down like a prospective customer in a slave market. It was unnerving the way this well-dressed man with his thinning blond hair and his glasses that reflected the harsh light of the courtroom looked at me. I could feel his eyes boring into me. Afterwards, he was to tell an Australian television documentary team that "I have the opportunity of looking these women in the eye, to size them up, and they don't appear to me to be incapable of doing a crime like this." For a professional lawyer who had originally offered to represent us before moving on to Frank Gilford as his second choice, it was an unnecessarily personal statement. After five minutes of that first court appearance Phipps stood up and read out a statement. All the proceedings up till then had been in Arabic and I could only pick out the occasional word or phrase. So it came as a complete shock to be able to understand him, like finding the right wavelength on a radio and a comprehensible message emerging suddenly pin-point sharp from the confusion of all the background static. In essence, Phipps said Frank Gilford was using his position as next of kin to demand his right under Islamic law for the death penalty to be imposed on his sister's murderers. We had suspected this was going to happen. We had been well warned when there had been no response to our lawyers' attempts to speak to Gilford himself. The real shock for us was to hear it spoken so bluntly with all the implications that went with it. I even have the idea that Phipps relished the words as he spoke them. Then he looked across at me as if to say, 'What do you think of that then?' No one had to tell us again that the death penalty in Saudi meant beheading in Chop Chop Square. As the interpreter translated Phipps's statement into Arabic for the benefit of the judges and the formal document was passed up to the table, Mike Dark leaned across to me and whispered: 'Don't worry. Stay calm. This still has a long way to go.' I had my hands clasped tightly together, the handcuffs digging into my wrists. I would have liked to have been brave enough to stare back into Phipps's eyes, but at that particular moment I didn't have the physical strength or the mental courage."

The Saudi defense team, assembled by Hejailan, began work immediately. Assisting Hejailan was Sir Michael Dark, at the time, an associate of the Hejailan law firm. Dark is experienced in English and international commercial transactions, litigation and arbitration, partnerships and joint ventures, corporate law, telecommunications, construction law and transactions. A British subject, residing and working as a lawyer in Romania, Dark holds degrees from Oxford University, and is admitted to the practice of law in England and Wales. Having worked nine years in Saudi Arabia, Sir Michael Dark is the senior English lawyer in the Kingdom of Saudi Arabia, and quite versed in Sharia law. According to Jon Ashbee and others close to the case, the well-respected Dark played a prominent role in defending the nurses.

On January 17, 1997, Michael Dark visited Lucille McLauchlan in prison. He asked her a number of questions about her arrest and association with Yvonne Gilford. As a defense attorney, he needed to extract as much information as possible, to reconstruct the case in an attempt to rebut the prosecution.

During the course of the interview, McLauchlan was asked a number of penetrating questions regarding her associations with the deceased. She explained she was checked for bruises and scratches two or three days after the murder, but none were found. The police searched her room two days after the murder, but no revealing evidence was discovered.

Dark asked her when the police first interviewed her, and McLauchlan stated it was the same night that Yvonne Gilford's body was found, with subsequent interviews over the next few days. McLauchlan told Dark that the police told her that it must have been at least two females who killed Gilford, due to evidence of a struggle.

The police continued with the theory that McLauchlan was the prime candidate since she reportedly was in Gilford's apartment the night of the murder, and her fingerprints were found. Dark asked McLauchlan about her theory as to why Yvonne Gilford was killed. McLauchlan explained Gilford was loaning money to people, and believed she *"stepped on someone else's toes."*

Another likely scenario, according to McLauchlan, was that security guards and a few Filipino girls were engaging in sex for money. Perhaps Gilford found out about the arrangement, and was eliminated for fear she would report them. Regarding the theory that a security guard may have killed her, McLauchlan admitted Gilford apparently had a peeping tom that was a security guard.

McLauchlan further informed Dark that Deslyn Marks, her nursing supervisor, continually stated from day one that, *"They, Lucille, Debbie, Olwyn and Carolyn, should all watch their friends closely because the police believed it was one or two of Yvonne's friends who committed the murder."*

Of course, McLauchlan wondered whether Marks came to this conclusion herself, or were the police behind this information? According to McLauchlan, Marks knew everything about the relations between the security guards and Filipino nurses.

On February 3, 1997, Michael Dark conducted a second interview at the prison, this time with both Lucille McLauchlan and Deborah Parry. Both nurses indicated that Yvonne Gilford's friends included: Carolyn, the Polish plaster technician; Michelle, an RNI; Colin Campbell, a lecturer in the hospital college; and Rory, a Filipino nurse in Male Specialty.

When asked about the alleged use of Gilford's bankcard, neither McLauchlan nor Parry admitted using the ATM card, nor was either aware if anyone else used Gilford's ATM card. They were both paid their salaries each month they worked at the hospital, and although the salaries may have been a few days late, they were never late enough to cause financial problems.

The only debt owed by Parry was a loan from the National Westminster Bank of Pounds Sterling 1,500. McLauchlan owed money to her father of which he kept a record, but he was not expecting to be repaid at any particular time. The only person they knew who owed money to Yvonne Gilford was a Filipino nurse named Teresita Balderama, who reportedly owed SR3,000.

Neither nurse admitted borrowing money from Yvonne Gilford or from anyone else, except that Lucille McLauchlan had borrowed SR200 for a few days on one occasion and Deborah Parry SR500 on one occasion shortly after coming to the hospital. According to the nurses, both debts were repaid.

In the interview, McLauchlan stated that *"On the evening of Wednesday, 11 December 1996, Yvonne had had the day off and I had been working. Yvonne came to my room at about 9:00 PM saying that she had locked her key in her room. When I left Yvonne's room later that evening, I left the spare key with her."* McLauchlan believes other nurses may also have had a spare key to Gilford's room, and some may have been in Yvonne Gilford's room before her on the afternoon/evening of Wednesday, 11 December, 1996.

Deborah Parry told Dark that on the morning of Thursday, 19 December, 1996, the day of the arrest, she was not in the bank, but inside the mall. Parry knew the bank to which Lucille McLauchlan had gone that morning. When arrested, McLauchlan did not remember using her own credit card to withdraw or to try to withdraw money from the bank branch.

As to written statements given to the police after their arrest, McLauchlan's first written statement was taken on the night of Thursday, 19 December, 1996, and the second was taken on Monday, 23 December, 1996. Parry recalled making a number of drafts, but the two finished statements were written on Monday, 23 December 1996.

McLauchlan told Dark that after the arrest she was forcibly taken to Yvonne Gilford's room on three occasions following the murder. The first occasion was on Friday, 13 December, 1996. The second occasion was on Sunday, 22 December, when the police took some still photographs of her in the room. The third occasion was when the police took a video of Lucille McLauchlan and Deborah Parry reenacting the murder. The police actually took two videos because they said the sound on the first video was indistinct.

Throughout the four months of court hearings beginning in January 1997, the nurses were allowed to speak before the court for only twenty minutes; they continually proclaimed that their confessions were coerced. Yet none of the evidence obtained by their lawyers was considered and they were continually frustrated in their attempts to contest what they describe as "grossly flawed" prosecution evidence. Apart from the twenty minutes when the women spoke, most court time over the ensuing months was spent looking at their confessions, and reviewing the rights of Frank Gilford, Yvonne's brother and heir.

It is not unusual for defendants to have little opportunity to speak before the Saudi court, which was a consistent complaint of the nurses.

Their defense appears limited to answering the judge or judges' questions. Yet, the Hejailan defense team recognized a number of contradictions, inconsistencies, and investigative problems with the case, particularly the police role in soliciting the nurses' confessions.

It was the police role that the Hejailan team focused most heavily on in the beginning. He believed the police blundered in their investigation, and raised a number of questions regarding their tactics and investigative procedures. He raised such questions as:

• Why were the nurses kept in police custody without being allowed any outside contact for seven days if they were willing to confess voluntarily?

• Several nurses when interviewed by the police following the murder were shown a broken length of cheap metal bracelet or necklace and were told that this had been found on the floor of Gilford's bedroom. Has the owner of the bracelet been found?

• Yvonne Gilford had lent relatively large amounts of money to other nurses in the hospital. What inquires have been made about this?

• Violence has been used on at least one occasion in the hospital in order to encourage repayment of a loan; have the police identified those involved?

• Several female nurses were pestered and harassed by the security guards and by some of the male employees in the hospital. Do the police have details of these incidents?

• There was an unsolved murder of a female nurse at the hospital two years prior to the nurses' arrival. Is it more likely that another murderer is on the loose?

• What happened to the security guard that was known to have harassed Yvonne Gilford in the weeks before her death?

• Yvonne Gilford and other nurses had their wallets stolen some weeks before the murder. Was Gilford's bankcard in her wallet when it was stolen?

Where is the evidence? Apparently, there was no attempt to gather evidence other than a confession. The evidence against the nurses before and through the entire trial was their retracted confessions. Hejailan prepared his defense around this fact, bringing on his next assault, the trustworthiness of the nurses' confessions.

Hejailan and his team recognized the problems of confessional justice, and the abuses that may arise from relying entirely on confessions. Hejailan took serious issue with confessional justice, declaring: "It is the worst and weakest form of evidence for several reasons, the most important of which is that it is against the nature of things." Hejailan questioned why anyone would confess to a crime unless they chose to boast of the crime or were mentally ill.

However, was there other evidence? In an interview with the British *Daily Telegraph* reported on May 21, 1998, Saudi Ambassador to Great Britain, Dr. Ghazi Algosaibi stated that *"proof other than confessions was presented during the trial."* The proof, however, was not publicly presented. Again, there is no adversarial process in Saudi Arabia, no right to cross examination, no right for the defense to attack or suppress evidence. This frustrated Hejailan and the defense.

For years Sharia scholars have recognized the limitations of confessions. Dr. Sami Sadiq Almula, a recognized Egyptian scholar stated the following in his 1962 book:

Whatever the guarantees regarding confessions provided in the laws of the civilized nations for the benefit of the accused, confession is still a type of evidence involving suspicion because it is related from the start with the idea of torture and inherent in the conflict of the accused's desire to escape punishment and to submit the evidence for his own conviction. Furthermore, confessions may be a manifestation of mental imbalance or psychological disturbance.

In a letter to the Supreme Sharia Court in Al-Khobar (see Appendix D), Hejailan requests the judges to consider the evidence of the accused. Hejailan not only attacks the police, but also questions the strength of the entire case against the nurses, especially the legitimacy of the confessions. In making his points, he cites the Koran, sayings of the prophet Mohammed (PBUH), Sharia law, and the Saudi constitution. His letter is a bold unprecedented attack on the evidence against the nurses.

Hejailan promotes the argument that the police interrogation did not follow procedural justice under Sharia law. He raises questions about human rights violations and injustice, which is a violation of the Saudi constitution (Article 26) regardless of the religious faith of the accused. Under Islam, everyone has a right to fair treatment. There is nothing in the Koran that says a believer of another faith will be treated with less care than a Muslim.

Hejailan points out that a confession absent other evidence is not sufficient to convict anyone of anything! Hejailan suggests that Sharia judges wake up and recognize that other evidence is needed to convict the nurses. If there was other evidence, as asserted by Dr. Algosaibi, the Saudi ambassador to Great Britain, then let's review it. Hejailan cites historical evidence that mistakes can be made by judges. If the police have done their homework, conducted a clean and thorough investigation, there will be enough evidence to convict.

All defense efforts were on the alleged confessions. There was some dispute as to who originated the confrontation leading to Gilford's death, and who initiated the lesbian relationship, if one in fact did occur. The judges were not swayed by Hejailan's eloquent arguments, at least officially or publicly.

However, one has to speculate on what the Sharia court really believed or understood. Hejailan was forcing the court to go against tradition, raising serious issues as to judicial decision-making practices, something Sharia judges are not accustomed to addressing. The court held several sessions after the nurses' first judicial appearance in January, 1997. True to form, there was little information released about the proceedings, or evidence against the accused.

But court silence can only last so long. On September 23, 1997, the Sharia court decreed that Lucille McLauchlan was guilty as an accessory to murder and sentenced to 500 lashes and eight years in prison. This long-awaited decision meant that the judges were convinced that McLauchlan was a bit player in the murder. This decision seems suspicious. Why was McLauchlan convicted first and then only as an accessory? Was there a deal made?

And what of Parry's fate? Rumors and unofficial reports circulated that Parry was found guilty of murder, and sentenced to death. Media sources reported that a judicial panel issued the verdict of death in late August or early September 1997. But no official public announcement was made.

If Parry was in fact found guilty of "intentional murder," a new twist had been added to the case. Only Parry was a candidate for beheading, not McLauchlan. This changed the strategy somewhat, and raised questions as to how McLauchlan got a lesser conviction, while Parry was to lose her head. What evidence was there to shift most of the blame to Parry?

This was especially suspicious since McLauchlan confessed long before Parry. Perhaps Hejailan's arguments had some merit after all, because now the degree of guilt between the nurses was different, future blood money negotiations would surely be affected.

For both McLauchlan and Parry, the next year would turn out to be an extraordinary nightmare. During the course of the trial, the nurses were confined to prison. For Debbie Parry, the incarceration was particularly painful, due to her fragile state of mind. Rumors of conviction and impending beheading were not exactly relaxation therapy strategies.

During their extensive incarceration, demands for the nurses' heads were heard from Frank Gilford and even Yvonne Gilford's mother, hospitalized with Alzheimer's disease. Mrs. Gilford broke her silence to speak for herself. The women, she declared, "Should die if found guilty." Mr. Gilford himself decreed: *"If a dog goes out and kills a mob of sheep, what do you do with it? You put it down so it cannot do it again."*

His plea was supported by a group of Yvonne's friends from South Africa, where she formerly worked. They urged Mr. Gilford, *"To see that her death is avenged with the ultimate penalty."* Both nurses waited and wondered what destiny awaited them. Except for periodic visits from family and lawyers, the nurses suffered through days of the idle confinement, ugly rumors, and an uncertain destiny.

In spite of the nurses' living in hideous conditions, a promising event transpired on November 30, 1997. Lucille McLauchlan was granted permission to marry Grant Ferrie in prison. Why would the Saudis allow this nuptial to take place if they planned to imprison her for a number of years. This event was a positive sign in the ordeal, an indication that the Saudis were softening their stance, or possibly events were turning in favor of the nurses.

The wedding was no cause for celebration by the defense team; the team was now preparing to move on to the next level—blood money negotiations. In other words, it appeared the battle was just beginning, since no formal agreement was arranged with the Gilford camp.

7

BLOOD MONEY

The conviction of McLauchlan as an accessory to murder left open the grave prospect that Parry's fate would be worse. Rumors circulated that her sentence was already signed, sealed, and ready for delivery in the form of decapitation. The time was ripe for key players to "get their heads together" and consider other options; blood money or diya was the next option.

Diya has its roots in Islamic Law and dates to the time of the Prophet Mohammed when there were many local families, tribes, and clans. The clans were nomadic and traveled extensively. The Prophet was able to convince several tribes to take a monetary payment for damage to the clan or tribe. This practice grew and now is an acceptable solution to some Qesas crimes.

Today, the offender pays the diya to the victim if he is alive. If the victim is dead, the money is paid to the victim's family or to the victim's tribe or clan. The assumption is that victims will be compensated for their loss. A stipulation for any blood money agreement is that it must be unanimous among the victimized family members. If one member disagrees, then no agreement is made, unless the stubborn member is somehow convinced otherwise. In other words, blood money is a form of compromise between the parties, reached through consensus.

While blood money has roots in Islamic law, England has used the concept differently. In 1692, the English parliament enacted the now infamous "Reward Statutes," promising cash rewards, known then as "Blood Money Certificates," to people providing the government with information leading to the conviction of criminals. But temptation gave way to abuse, and the statutes were repealed in the mid 1750s after it was discovered a group of career informants had framed innocent people (some of whom were executed) in order to collect the cash rewards.

In Western society, we still employ bounty hunters who scour the planet, seeking renegades wanted for crimes. Reward money is still alive and well and often needed to motivate. Under common law systems of the United States and England, blood money is not an option to replace execution. Most murderers have no funds, nor do their families (if they have any) have funds to fulfill any blood money arrangement. The victim or family must sue the offender in a civil tort action for damages incurred from the crime, such as pain and suffering, distress, and so forth.

In other words, the Western equivalent to a blood money arrangement is a civil suit where the victim's family may file a claim against the murderer with the hope of winning civil damages. The suit, if successful, is a form of compensation for the suffering experienced by the victim's family. But the offender may still be criminally punished and even executed, or may remain criminally innocent.

One example of this process is the well-publicized O.J. Simpson trial. Although the former American football star was acquitted of a criminal conviction, he was found guilty in a civil judgment and sentenced to pay twenty-eight million dollars for the wrongful death of Ronald Goldman and former spouse Nicole Brown Simpson. Some say the civil judgment was a form of blood money.

What happens to the debt if the offender dies and has not paid it? Historically, it was passed on to the offender's heirs; today, most nations terminate the debt if the offender left no inheritance. One question that is often raised in Saudi Arabia is What happens if a victim takes the diya without government approval? The victim or family has committed a Tazir crime by accepting money, which was not mandated by a judge. Taking diya must be carried out through proper governmental and judicial authority.

The Quesas crimes require compensation for each crime committed. If an offender is too poor to pay the diya, the family of the offender is called upon next to make good the diya for their kin. If the family is unable to pay, the community, clan or tribe may be required to pay. This concept is not found in common law or the civil law of most nations.

Another concept of Queses crimes is punishment. Each victim has the right to ask for retaliation and, historically, the victim's family would carry out that punishment. Modern Islamic law now requires the government to carry out the Quesas punishment. Historically, some grieving family member may have tortured the offender in the process of punishment. Now the government is the independent party that administers the punishment, because torture and extended pain is contrary to Islamic teachings and Sharia Law.

In the event of a conviction and possibility of execution, the defense task is to negotiate for blood money. In the Gilford murder, it appeared that this dreadful likelihood arrived, since McLauchlan was convicted as an accessory to murder, and unofficial reports circulated that Parry was convicted of murder. This is another mystery of the case. Nothing official was every presented by the court indicating either of the nurses were convicted. It was as if everything was taken for granted or left for a conjecture.

For months, Hejailan's team realized the Gilford heirs might seek the death penalty if the nurses were found guilty of intentional murder, a Queses crime. The statements of Frank Gilford suggest that he sought revenge, payback for his sister's death.

Notwithstanding the confrontation, this is the right of the murdered victim's family to seek vengeance, grant forgiveness, or accept a financial settlement known as blood money. However, any demand for death must be unanimous by the family members. If there are no living relatives, guardians may be appointed by the court.

Along with the private right is the public right of justice, which is police prosecution. If the nurses were convicted of intentional murder and the family waived the death penalty, the nurses could still be sent to prison for a period, usually up to eight years.

Frank Gilford always believed that a prison sentence was too merciful. He was quoted in the early stages of the case as saying that, if the nurses were granted clemency, they would escape with light penalties. Hejailan found Gilford's behavior and untimely media comments reprehensible. On one hand Gilford was openly critical of the Saudi system, but on the other, he was willing to cash in on the benefits of blood money.

Defending the case was becoming more problematic. But the task was clear: identify Yvonne Gilford's heirs, determine their competence, and if necessary, negotiate for forgiveness or blood money. Of course, there was the remote chance the court might agree that the nurses' confessions were the product of the alleged torture and abuse and find in their favor. And there was the possibility that the crime did not rise to the level of intentional murder and not subject to punishment by death. It was an unprecedented case in many respects, posing unusual problems, both politically, systematically, emotionally.

The first hurdle for the defense was to attack the nurses' confessions; but on what grounds could the confessions, supposedly given under duress, be retracted? Hejailan believed the confessions were the product of duress, and was out to prove it.

In a defense brief written by Hejailan on March 25, 1997, entitled <u>Reason for retraction of the confessions</u>, he offers reasoning to the court as to why the nurses' confessions should be retracted. This is Hejailan's second attempt to convince the court to conclude that the nurses' confessions were unreliable.

As explained by the accused in the previous hearings, they have retracted their confessions for the following reasons:

- *These confessions have been obtained under duress and oppression.*
- *The confessions have been obtained under threat of rape. As explained by the two nurses and confirmed by the report prepared by the fiancé of Lucille McLauchlan, the acts of the investigators amounted to an attempt to commit rape.*
- *These confessions have been obtained in response to a promise by the investigators to discharge both of the accused and send them home within a period of two weeks.*
- *These confessions have been obtained against a confirmation that both of the accused being non-Muslims would not be subject to the punishment prescribed by Sharia Law.*

These reasons mentioned by both accused are deemed by Sharia Law to constitute duress and oppression.

Under the established Sharia principles an accused person is entitled to retract his confession in case it has been proved that such confession had been obtained under duress or threat of violence. The court has discretion to consider all the relevant circumstances in order to ascertain the accuracy or inaccuracy of the statements given by the accused. It is to be pointed out in this respect that the alleged confession was based on an alleged lesbian relationship between the deceased and each of the accused. The brother of the deceased, the fiancé of Lucille McLauchlan, and both accused as well as their colleagues have all denied the existence of such relationship. In these circumstances, the burden of proof shifts to the prosecution.

It is to be reiterated that the least doubt in criminal cases generally, and particularly in offenses against the human body, has to be interpreted in favor of the accused.

As compared with males, females are generally more responsive to duress and oppression. Accordingly, it would not be unsound for a female who is kept in custody before her trial for a charge of murder, or who has suffered a lot from repeated threat of violence and denied her lawful right to seek legal advice, to believe that she would be discharged if she confessed of a guilt which she has not committed, specially where such female belongs to a different culture where different religious creed, intellectual background and social habits prevail. In these circumstances, it would not be hard to believe the promises made to her and to write on paper whatever she is asked to write in the hope that her sufferings would come to an end. We believe that the court will consider all these circumstances before judging on the admissibility or inadmissibility of the said confessions.

Hejailan argued that the nurses were coerced and under duress, implying that under these cruel circumstances anyone, especially women surrounded by six police officers, will say anything. This may sound somewhat sexist to the Westerner, but it does make sense to Saudis. Saudi Arabia is a male-dominated society, where women have few public rights. Additionally, we have two Western women detrained for several days in an unfavorable if not hostile environment thousands of miles from home. Clearly, this was not merry old England, or an environment championing the cause for feminism.

However, with McLauchlan's conviction, it appeared that the Sharia judges were not convinced the confessions resulted from abuse or torture. Maybe they had other information, or maybe they didn't care. In the close Saudi judicial system there are no public records of judicial decisions. In any event, Hejailan and his team was forced to resort to another plan.

As with the principle that the best offense is a good defense, the defense team prepared an alternate strategy. In anticipation of the worst scenario, a death sentence, Hejailan crafted an eloquent argument addressing the uniqueness of the case, attacking the evidence, and the death penalty. Termed the Rationale of Early Waiver of the Death Penalty (see Appendix B), the document requested the court and Gilford heirs to seriously question the strength of the case against the nurses, and the imposition of any sentence in the event the nurses were convicted of intentional murder.

The waiver, written by Hejailan on March 27, 1997, was probably the most important defense appeal written on behalf of the nurses. Why was it important? It was a rational attack on the death penalty. Hejailan understood that the death penalty is not used in many countries, most notably the United Kingdom and Australia. Death, the extreme form of retribution, does not solve anything. He further addressed the differences between the Saudi and Western approach to resolving truth.

Some criticized Hejailan for writing the waiver. It read like an admission of guilt, as if the defense was throwing in the towel in the middle of the fight. However, to Hejailan, the document was designed to bolster the defense by discussing the weaknesses of the case, and appealing to Gilford to consider such weaknesses. Given the weak evidence and retracted confessions of the nurses, the waivers called for Gilford to exercise mercy in the event the nurses were in fact guilty of intentional murder.

A further purpose of the document was to appeal directly to the Gilford family to waive the death penalty. Hejailan sought to force Gilford to make a decision early. It is a finely-tuned philosophical and legal argument written in a style fit for a college classroom. But it is one of many strategies Hejailan chose to keep the executioner away from the nurses.

Another strategy utilized by the defense was to examine the competency of the Gilford heirs. Yvonne Gilford had two heirs, her mother Muriel Gilford, and brother Frank Gilford, both living in Australia. However, Yvonne Gilford bequeathed very little to her brother. In her will, Gilford left her flat and some insurance bonds to the two children of a nurse she had previously worked with. It is believed she left money to a godson in New Zealand.

If there are no heirs, or if the heirs are mentally incompetent, death cannot be imposed. Based on various press releases, information surfaced that Muriel Gilford was suffering from Alzheimer's disease, and confined to a nursing home in Adelaide, Australia. This revelation piqued the interest of the defense team. If true, then the only remaining heir was Frank Gilford, who already was calling for the nurses' heads. This would mean that he would be the only person to do business with, and he might not be in a legitimate position to demand death.

Getting cooperation from the lawyers representing the Gilford family was another matter. There were problems in communications. It was known that an American lawyer, James Phipps, working for the Gilford team, traveled to Australia to meet with Frank Gilford. It was entirely possible he had knowledge about Muriel Gilford's condition, and was playing a legal cat and mouse game in an attempt to up the ante. Phipps was associated with an American law firm, which had connections with the Saudi firm of Osama Al-Solaim.

It is common for law firms in Saudi Arabia, including Hejailan's firm, to have ties with Western law firms due to international business ventures and so forth. However, the Hejailan team did not welcome the involvement of another firm, believing that the firm was out to capitalize on the case.

It seemed that litigation and lawyers were oozing out from all over the globe. Yet one way to fight lawyers is with more lawyers. Realizing little information was coming forth to verify Muriel Gilford was in fact incompetent, Hejailan retained the services of Minter, Ellison, Baker, O'Loughlan, a law firm in Adelaide, Australia. In a letter dated 30 July, 1997 to Andrew Short of the Australian law firm, Michael Dark requested assistance in establishing the mental competency of Muriel Gilford. Hejailan's attempt was to determine if Gilford's mother was competent. If not, this would block any attempt by Frank Gilford to demand death, since there must be consensus by all family members.

Dear Mr. Short,

We are representing two British nurses who are on trial for murder in Saudi Arabia. The two nurses are called Lucille McLauchlan and Deborah Parry. The two nurses have pleaded not guilty and deny any involvement in the death of the victim, Yvonne Gilford, who was an Australian nurse working in the same hospital.

Under Shari'a law, which is the Islamic religious law which is applied in these cases, the heirs of the deceased may have the right to demand the death penalty if the accused are found guilty. The heirs of Yvonne Gilford are her mother, Muriel Gilford, and her brother, Frank Gilford.

We understand that Muriel Gilford is suffering from Alzheimer's disease and is being cared for in a nursing home in Adelaide. Unfortunately, we do not know the address of the nursing home. Frank Gilford lives in Jamestown, north of Adelaide.

Under Shari'a law it may be that if we can prove to the court that Muriel Gilford is not mentally competent then it will not be possible for the court to impose the death penalty.

At the last hearing on 27 July 1997 the court adjourned the case until 10 August 1997 to give us an opportunity to obtain evidence that Muriel Gilford is not mentally competent. We have written to the lawyers in Saudi Arabia who are representing the heirs and a copy of that letter follows. We think it probable that those lawyers will not provide us with the information we have requested.

In the circumstances, we wish to explore some other way of obtaining the evidence we need. The only two possibilities that have occurred to us are to obtain an affidavit from the director of the nursing home and/or, preferably, to seek assistance from the court in Adelaide to obtain disclosure of Muriel Gilford's recent medical reports.

Could you please let us know if you would be able to assist us in this matter and, if so, the likely costs involved. We are assuming that we will be able to obtain an adjournment at the next hearing if necessary.

I will telephone you tomorrow morning, my time, to discuss this matter with you.

Yours sincerely,
Michael Dark
The Law Firm of Salah Al-Hejailan

A few weeks later, the Australian courts decreed Muriel Gilford was not a competent heir. Therefore, the only person left to deal with was Frank Gilford. And it was becoming evident to the defense that the Gilford legal team, and Frank Gilford in particular, was out for blood money, which of course is his right. Normally, a consensus of all family members is needed to demand death, but in this case the sole remaining competent male family member can demand the penalty

The Gilford team rejected outright Hejailan's <u>Rationale for Early Waiver of the Death Penalty</u>. Gilford was not swayed by the finely-tuned document, and instead, made public statements supporting the beheading of the nurses if they were found guilty. Retribution, not compassion, was on the mind of Gilford.

The media was in a feeding frenzy over Gilford's punitive stance, and questions persisted that he might be doing this intentionally (with his lawyers) to raise the blood money stakes. A dreadful but business-like decision, if true.

All this wavering and dawdling and legal chicanery was beginning to infuriate the nurses. They were confused, exposed to all sorts of ugly gossip and rumors, with information coming from radio broadcasts and visits from relatives and lawyers. They painfully recognized Gilford was out for blood. The gamesmanship definitely took a toll on the mental health of the nurses, particularly Deborah Parry. They considered suing the Cleveland firm, Frank Gilford, and others for exacerbating their plight, and ignoring the Islamic tradition of "reconciliation."

After a month of stalling by the Gilford team and his reported ill-timed predictions of Parry's possible death by beheading, it was time for Hejailan to come to an agreement. The thought of surrendering your head is not particularly appealing even if the statement wasn't true.

Reports circulated that Parry found it difficult to cope with life in prison. There were reports Parry tried to commit suicide where she'd been held for the past 13 months, and doctors decided to move her to a hospital for observation as a precautionary measure. Relatives said her spirits had been sinking lower and lower as time went on, and the doctors had decided to keep a constant watch on her.

McLauchlan described in her dairies how Parry's bizarre behavior was becoming a problem. She described Parry as *"having mood swings, taking medication causing her to sleep 11-12 hours a day, and generally becoming a pain in the ass."*

Fellow Hejailan defense lawyer Robert Thoms, a close associate of Hejailan, and a Harvard man to boot, got into the affray. The intelligent, quick-witted attorney was quoted as saying: *"Gilford's intemperate behavior is making a circus of the case. People have this image of Saudis as being backward and bloodthirsty and cutting heads off right and left, if these ladies ever face the ultimate penalty, it's not because of the Saudis; it's because of this Australian man."*

Pressure was beginning to mount against Frank Gilford from political sources to disregard the death penalty. Australia's foreign minister Alexander Downer said Australia wanted justice for the killing of an Australian citizen but opposed the death penalty. "Our first priority has been that whoever it was that murdered an Australian citizen must be brought to justice, (but) the Australian government does not support capital punishment," he was quoted as saying.

Australian legal advisors to Frank Gilford did not want to see Deborah Parry beheaded. As explained in Hejailan's defense waiver, Australia and the United Kingdom did not apply the death penalty in capital murder cases. Since there was an element of doubt as to the reliability of the nurses' confessions and there was no other evidence presented before the court indicating guilt, pressure was on Gilford to accept blood money.

Due to the urging from political sources both in Australia and the United Kingdom, Gilford realized that blood money was the best recourse. In September, 1997, after intensive and unusually prolonged negotiations, Frank Gilford signed a deed of settlement for blood money. During this period, Great Britain and Saudi Arabia were negotiating an arms and fighter aircraft deal reportedly worth millions of dollars. The case was no longer just about two nurses embroiled in a murder and sex tale, but had much deeper international implications.

Before any deal could be approved, the nurses had to agree. On September 22, 1997, both nurses signed an agreement under protest, maintaining their innocence, but gaining their long-awaited freedom. The agreements addressed to one of the lawyers, Roger Pannone, are printed below.

Dear Sir Roger,

I am opposed to signing this settlement document, as I am totally innocent, and it is abhorrent to me to give so much money to someone in connection with a crime that I did not commit. But in the circumstances, I have no choice but to sign, because the threat of the death penalty is too much for me to bear.

My family and I have suffered enormous mental torment already by virtue of the death threat that has been unjustly hanging over me for what seems a lifetime and that has been prolonged and worsened by the actions of Mr. Gilford and his lawyers.

Despite the injustice of this agreement, as a nurse I am pleased that at least some of the money will go to the hospital in Adelaide, and would prefer that the entire sum be given to charity. However, as with the threat of the death penalty, I am in the hands of Mr. Gilford and of whatever his demands may be as to who will be the ultimate recipient of the funds.

I would like to state here and now that I append my signature with a totally clear conscience, in the full and certain knowledge that I am innocent of the unsubstantiated charges against me.

I note sadly that Mr. Gilford has only agreed to join us in asking the

Saudi Arabian authorities to disclose all the evidence in their possession relating to the murder after he has been paid.
Yours sincerely, Deborah K. Parry, 22nd September 1997

McLauchlan's letter was nearly identical to Parry's.

Dear Sir Roger,
I am writing this from Dammam Central Prison whilst I await a verdict on the outcome of my trial of the murder of Yvonne Gilford.
Although I am signing this document, I do so with great reluctance, and I sincerely hope that my signature will not be misinterpreted by the Saudi Arabian authorities and others as in any way being an admission of guilt. I have no choice but to settle privately with Mr. Gilford for money, and however distasteful, I am under enormous pressure to do so.
The constant threat of the unjust death penalty has caused unbelievable stress and worry, not only to Debbie and myself, but also to our families and friends and to our supporters who have done so much to Help us for no financial gain.
I am innocent of all charges against me and hope and pray that I have the chance of a fair trial to clear my name in the future.
I have from the beginning asked Mr. Gilford to help us in finding out the truth regarding Yvonne's death, but only now has he agreed to join us in uncovering the evidence—upon his receipt of a small fortune. It is a cruel world that ties our search for justice to someone else's mercenary aims, but there seems to be no escaping that cynical equation.
I hope that any money which Mr. Gilford receives from this settlement or which he manages to raise himself from this tragedy will be used in a charitable way in memory of his sister, my colleague and friend, Yvonne. Let us hope that it is in the memory of the charity, which lasts, not the aftertaste of the other money which will be passed.
Yours sincerely, Lucille McLauchlan

The dust had not settled yet. In a press release issued on September 22, 1997, Hejailan criticized Frank Gilford for dragging the negotiations over several months.
"The announcement made earlier today in Adelaide by Frank Gilford that he has executed a Special Power of Attorney waiving his rights as an heir under Saudi Arabian law to demand the death penalty was long overdue. The proper time for him to have made such an announcement would have been either in response to the Rationale for Early Waiver of the Death Penalty, which was presented to him by our law firm for his thoughtful consideration in March, 1997 but which he instead instantly trashed in a campaign he has been until recently waging to condemn the

*nurses, or at the latest when, on the basis of the Deed of Settlement which
he signed on 19 September, 1997, the Settlement Sum was deposited in full
into the Trust Account on 1 October, 1997."*

The Saudi Arabian court would adjust the amount paid to Frank
Gilford. He had no right under Saudi law to demand or receive any
money from Lucille McLauchlan since her conviction was for a lesser
crime than intentional murder. Furthermore, payment of any "blood
money" for Deborah Parry would have to await her conviction.

As for the nature of any payment which was to be made to Frank
Gilford under the Deed of Settlement, it is clear from the document that
the payment was "blood money" and not, as Frank Gilford later argued,
a type of compensation. Gilford tried to draw a distinction between
"blood money," which he said is for a prescribed amount in Saudi Arabia,
versus "compensation" which he said is open-ended. There is, however,
no substance to this distinction. In truth, Frank Gilford was to receive a
very large amount of "blood money." The Deed of Settlement compensated Frank Gilford for his "right as an heir," and that is "blood money."

Frank Gilford was confused about the differences between compensation, which was "pain and suffering," and blood money. Hejailan was
also baffled why Gilford thought he should be compensated for his having sensationalized the case for so many months. The nurses, as argued
by Hejailan, suffered immensely by sitting in prison for months; they
heard rumors of their death, while waiting for Gilford to agree on a blood
money deal.

Gilford's legal fees were escalating, which may be another reason to
seek a resolution. There are those who believe that if Frank Gilford had
acted properly and at the appropriate time, his legal fees would have
been minimal.

Debate surfaced as to when Gilford formally agreed to waive his right
of death. According to Hejailan, Frank Gilford effectively waived his right
to demand the death penalty when he engaged in serious negotiations
over money, not later. Frank Gilford went beyond that when he signed
the Deed of Settlement on 19 September, 1997. But why the delay in
announcing his decision? The delay, according to Hejailan, was for
Gilford to make some more money.

It was not until November 16, 1997 that Gilford formally accepted
blood money in lieu of allowing the beheading of Deborah Parry. Frank
Gilford agreed to drop his insistence on the death penalty in return for
around £680,000 (1.2m Australian dollars).

But who would pay? The British government would not take funds
from the public treasury to pay the blood money. However, British aero-
space firms wanted a pending aircraft deal with the Saudis to go forward.
Approximately 50 fighter aircraft were scheduled for Saudi delivery. To

assure nothing would jeopardize the deal, the companies allegedly raised the money on behalf of the nurses. However, this deal was never publicly disclosed and to this day is merely a strong assertion, although a good one. During these exhausting negotiations, tensions were growing between the defense team as well. On July 28, 1998, an interview with Rodger Panonne, a lawyer for Parry, also working pro bono for the nurses, revealed miscommunications between the lawyers representing the nurses.

To some, it was becoming evident that Hejailan was interfering with the negotiations, and was more concerned with upgrading his importance in the case, rather than trying to resolve the matter. The plan to pay Gilford $1.2 million to exercise his right as brother of the deceased to waive the death penalty had gone wrong. A problem arose when Salah Al-Hejailan exposed the deal to the world's media. When Al-Hejailan told the press about the deal, Gilford threatened to withdraw his waiver offer unless Parry and McLauchlan issued a press release by 7 a.m. British time refuting the comments. He faxed his own press release refuting the Saudi lawyer's comments Gilford originally insisted on a confidentiality clause in the agreement. Gilford then gave Parry and McLauchlan eight weeks to raise the money, to be transferred to a trust account.

A leading respected personal injury lawyer and former law society President from Manchester, England, Pannone was suddenly thrust into dealing with a strange legal system and countless officials. He, like Michael Dark, played a critical role in the case, and, like Dark, probably didn't receive (nor did he seek) the publicity and media exposure other parties seemed to savor. But as described by Jon Ashbee, it was Pannone who was most available and supportive during the dark days of confinement of his sister-in-law, Deborah Parry.

Parry and McLauchlan's Australian lawyer, Michael Burnett, described the tension. "We had to be very cautious with everything we did because we could not have been playing for higher stakes than the lives of the women." Burnett faxed back to Al-Hejailan informing him that he intended to transfer the money as requested by Parry and McLauchlan. Al-Hejailan then issued a press release, stating he authorized Burnett to transfer the money to Gilford fifteen minutes after the money had actually been released.

Confusion between the lawyers was played out against a delicate international situation over the nurses' arrest. The English Lawyers were often furious if not confused about Hejailan's behavior but were forced to placate him. Both Pannone and Burnett believed Hejailan was directing the case for publicity reasons, assuming all the credit, and basking in the glow of international media attention. These accusations ruffled Hejailan. Not known for timidity, Hejailan wrote a steaming letter to

Pannone and Watson defending his position and tactics used. In the March 13, 1997 letter, Hejailan outlines seven points as to his role in the case. The letter is presented in its entirety (Appendix C) to indicate that a rift was apparent between the lawyers. The letter by Hejailan may be viewed as a way to save face, an effort to clarify his role in the delicate blood money negotiations, or an effort to keep everyone on track or to use a sports phrase, "on the same page."

Yet, Pannone refused to be drawn into the ongoing controversy. He supported Hejailan's importance in securing Parry and McLauchlan's release as the only lawyer on the team who fully understood the Saudi criminal legal system. In addition, Hejailan and Sir Michael Dark were the only lawyers in direct contact with the nurses. Furthermore, it made no sense to debate with each other at time when lives were at stake, and reputations on the line.

Further tensions erupted on the day the money reached Gilford. Hejailan faxed Burnett at the eleventh hour instructing him not to transfer the money to Gilford, although the nurses' lawyers refuse to spell out why. Hejailan claimed Burnett had authorization to act on his instructions only. In fact, the relationship between the two was very different. Hejailan was Parry and McLauchlan's lawyer in Saudi Arabia, but both Burnett and Pannone acted for Parry, and in Burnett's case, McLauchlan, outside Saudi jurisdiction.

Although a Saudi court convicted the pair (although it is not clear as to the exact date of judgment), Frank Gilford had not received any money when the women were released from jail and returned to Britain in May 1998. Salah Hejailan said the cash, put up by UK firms with trade ties to Saudi Arabia, would not be handed to Gilford until he publicly admitted it was "blood money," not compensation.

8

ҺOMEWARD BOUND

On May 18, 1998, King Fahd commuted the nurses' sentence to time served. The nurses served seventeen months for their murder convictions, McLauchlan for accessory to murder and Parry for murder. Not an excessive punishment considering that in most any other country, a convicted murderer can expect death, life, or a significant number of years behind bars.

Although their prison ordeal was finally over, it will not be forgotten. The sentence reduction is not an admission of innocence, for the nurses remain guilty under Saudi law for the murder of Yvonne Gilford. Saudi Ambassador to Great Britain, Ghazi Algosaibi, said in a news release that Deborah Parry and Lucille McLauchlan had their sentences commuted on humanitarian grounds. It is also believed that the visit of British Prime Minister Tony Blair to King Fahd in April, 1998 assisted the release. King Fahd respected Blair, and wanted relations between the two nations intact.

The King's action was "as an act of mercy" in response to the petition presented by the two women and because the victim's next of kin had waived his right to retribution. It would serve no purpose to detain the nurses after a blood money agreement had been reached. Neither the United Kingdom nor the Desert Kingdom would benefit from the continued confinement of the nurses.

An additional consideration for their early release was the fact that the nurses were Westerners (non-Muslims). Would they be released if they were Filipino or African? Probably not, or at least not as quickly. Let's face it, economics and politics are part of the justice equation. Yet, for the record, the Saudis deny that the decision to release the nurses was based purely on politics.

On May 21, 1998, wearing abayas over their Western clothing, the nurses boarded a British Airways jet for their five-hour flight home. When Lucille McLauchlan and Deborah Parry's plane landed at Gatwick Airport, an army of reporters met them. Exhausted from their trip and instructed not to conduct interviews, the women left the airport swiftly and separately.

Finally, their ordeal was over. They were rid of the Saudis, and the Saudis were equally delighted at the separation. But what did they return to? McLauchlan awaited criminal charges in Scotland for theft. Deborah Parry's mental health was questionable. Would they be able to rebuild their lives? Start over? While both nurses have their supporters, there are those who believe they are guilty.

An immediate concern for the nurses was their continued work as health professionals. Upon arriving home, the United Kingdom Central Council for Nursing was preparing to launch an investigation into Deborah Parry and Lucille McLauchlan after receiving a formal complaint against them from the Scottish Labour Parliament member, George Galloway, a critic of the nurses.

Galloway questions their right to work as nurses after being convicted of murder. In a news quote to the Guardian on May 22, 1998, Galloway asserts:

"Notwithstanding any opposition I have to the regime in Saudi Arabia, the facts are that the evidence against these women is extremely powerful and serious. Even though the conviction occurred abroad it is nonetheless a conviction and should at the very least be investigated before they are allowed to practice as nurses."

Despite the barrage of criticism, on Monday September 14, 1998, Parry began work as a nurse at Holy Cross Hospital in Hastemere, Surry. Parry had worked at the hospital in 1982.

Both cut deals to sell their stories to newspapers. It was reported that McLauchlan's husband, Grant Ferrie, entered negotiations with several newspapers for the story of his romance with Lucille McLauchlan. Much of the information about their experiences comes from diaries kept by the nurses and statements from Ferrie.

The Mirror is understood to have paid more than £100,000 for exclusive rights to McLauchlan's story, while the Express paid £60,000 in a deal with Parry. Both women used the newspaper deals to reveal their hatred of the Saudi regime and protest their innocence.

Should convicted offenders be allowed to profit from crimes? Does it matter if they're convicted in a foreign country or not? In the United States, convicted offenders are not allowed to profit from their crimes. If they write a book, proceeds go to the victim's family, not to the criminal.

Many in the United Kingdom agree the nurses should not benefit financially from their experiences. Again, George Galloway takes the opportunity to blast the decision to pay the nurses for their stories, arguing in a news release, *"Criminals are not supposed to profit from their crimes."*

In the au pair case discussed in chapter one, Louise Woodward is not permitted to gain financially from the crime. Despite her protested innocence, she is still guilty under American law. Of course, the media justification for printing the stories about the nurses was to prove to the public they were innocent. The stories, whether believed or not, are sensational, provocative, and newsworthy. In the United Kingdom, as long as the stories serve a public interest there is nothing illegal about the payment.

Parry is planning a television drama. News reports indicate that Parry and her brother-in-law, Jonathan Ashbee, are in negotiations with television companies to discuss theories as to who killed Yvonne Gilford.

There's no denying that the nurses suffered a great deal, and their friendship, if one truly existed, was damaged. Tension between the nurses was obvious. In an interview after their return, Parry described the difference between her and McLauchlan as "chalk and cheese." While going their separate ways, they continued to hurl insults at each other through the media. Parry has been called a snob, and McLauchlan termed a liar.

Feeling betrayed, Parry blamed McLauchlan for tricking her into confessing. *"I was so stupid at the beginning to rely on Lucy. I listened to her too much when she told me that I would be home in just two weeks if I confessed."*

McLauchlan counters Parry's accusation: "It was as if Debbie wanted someone to blame," she says. "And it was easier for her to blame me for signing a confession than face up to the situation. From that moment, though, there was even more resentment and distress between us." She admits, as does Parry, that at times they "intensely disliked" each other.

After the women returned to Britain, the case continued to inspire blame, insult, and to some extent revenge. At first, the governments of Britain and Saudi Arabia exchanged slaps about justice and human rights. Then the lawyers got into a squabble over blood money. In the end, we have the two nurses sparring with each other. Parry, upset about media reports, is considering suing for libel over <u>Death of a Sister</u>, a Channel 4 British documentary of the case, which suggested she (Parry) was the leading suspect. To add to the turmoil, Hejailan, on behalf of the nurses, threatened to sue Frank Gilford for prolonging blood money negotiations.

According to Hejailan, the excessive dilly-dallying of Gilford and his lawyers during the prolonged blood money negotiations caused severe hardship to the nurses. Hejailan compared their ordeal to "blackmail" orchestrated by the "greedy" Gilford team. It is not uncommon for criminals—and the nurses are convicted criminals under Saudi law—to denounce each other after apprehension. Criminals in general like to float reasons for their deviant antisocial behavior by blaming others, or minimize their involvement through a myriad of silly excuses.

It is difficult for convicted offenders to actually admit guilt. If you speak with enough convicts, there are no shortages of reasons for their criminal lifestyles. Excuses range from abusive childhood, stress, the moon's gravitational pull, too much sugar in the diet, PMS, mental disorder, failure to make the soccer team as a child, TV violence, devil worship, self defense, associating with the wrong crowd, drugs, sex, rock and roll, and so forth.

It is a common defense mechanism to point the finger at another to save a little face or butt depending upon what the direction you're facing.

While both nurses sold their stories to the tabloids, Lucille McLauchlan wrote a book titled Trial by Ordeal: My Life in a Saudi Jail. It was the first of several books on the case. The 223-page book is an account of her experiences in Saudi prison. The major thrust of the book is her day-to-day experiences in jail, and attacks on Deborah Parry, Frank Gilford, and Saudi justice.

The book is light reading. It is a diary, with harsh commentary about the Saudi justice system. I do not blame Lucille for the attacks: prison anywhere is a miserable environment. But most of her commentary focuses on lesbian inmates, "guards bonking female prisoners," her boredom and irregular menstrual cycles, bouts of diarrhea, her love for Grant Ferrie, Deborah Parry's depression and childlike antics, crappy Arab television, angry prisoners, and lack of recreation.

The problem with writing a book is that its contents can used for or against the writer. The book was written to give McLauchlan's side of the story and make a few pounds in the process. The one-sided rendering is full of quotes and anecdotal information.

Let's explore some of the contents. First, it is interesting that the repressive Saudi captors allowed Lucille McLauchlan to keep a diary in prison. If the Saudis were worried about repercussions, then why would they allow her to record evidence against them? Her book contained pictures from inside the prison. How were they obtained?

One could easily criticize McLauchlan for playing the totally innocent victim. Will Deborah Parry write a book rebutting McLauchlan's scurrilous comments toward her? The book certainly annoyed Frank Gilford. After her release, McLauchlan attempted to meet with Frank Gilford. He flatly refused saying, *"She is guilty. After all the nasty things that she said about me in the paper I have got no intentions of meeting with her. She is out to get publicity for the book she has recently written."*

McLauchlan faced other problems upon her arrival home. In 1996, prior to her work in Saudi Arabia and while a nurse at King's Cross Hospital in Dundee, Scotland, she was accused of stealing the money of an elderly patient and forging employment references. After her return and a two-day trial in December 1998, she was convicted. Her punishment, in addition to community service, was to pay £300 in compensation. The evidence against McLauchlan for her 1996 crime was direct. She was caught on a bank security camera stealing £300 from the account of a 79-year-old dying patient.

What about the man from down under? What did he get out of all this? The Gilford family received two cheques—one for or more than £400,000 (pounds), with which they built a ward at the Adelaide Women's and Children's Hospital dedicated to Yvonne's memory; and another for $700,000 Australian (£280,000), payable to a trust account administered by Gilford's lawyers.

Gilford will deduct $50,000 Australian (20,000 pounds) for expenses incurred since his sister's murder. His mother, who lives in a home for the elderly, will receive A$9,000 (£3,600). The remaining A$641,000 (£296,000) will pay legal bills. It is reported that when all was said and done, Frank Gilford received less than A$30,000 himself, but enough to put a few shrimps on the old barbie!

9
JUDGMENT

Did one or both of the nurses murder Yvonne Gilford on that fateful December evening? Maybe they did, but if so, was it self-defense? Perhaps someone else committed the murder. Could it have been a security guard, another co-worker, an irate loanshark, or unknown stalker? Are the nurses factually guilty? Factually innocent? Legally innocent? What does all this mean?

Legal innocence is when the offender actually committed the crime but was not convicted due to a technicality or mistake in the investigation process. The offender is factually guilty, but the case was not proven. In such cases, the police blundered or the evidence gathered was improperly admitted leading to an acquittal. If this occurs, the offender, for all practical purposes, has gotten away with murder.

If there is an element of doubt, or lack of evidence, the court must acquit. As opined by the infamous British Legalist Sir William Blackstone, *"It is better that ten guilty persons escape than one innocent suffer."* The French Philosopher Voltaire echoes Blackstone's argument, *"It is better to risk saving a guilty person than to condemn an innocent one."* We could apply these thoughts in the Gilford case because there are doubts raised about the factual guilt of both nurses. But, are there enough doubts raised to dismantle the case, and set them free?

Factual innocence, on the other hand, is when the offender did not commit the crime, despite evidence to the contrary. Sometimes the truly innocent are convicted of crimes they did not commit. Their convictions resulted from bogus testimony, mistaken identity, poor defense, or a corrupt justice process. Unfortunately, most persons victimized by this injustice are usually poor or of a minority class.

It is accurate to say that a number of poor souls have served time in prison or even been executed for crimes they did not commit. It is estimated that one percent of all convicted persons in American prisons are factually innocent. While this number may seem small, it translates to thousands of innocent persons serving time for major crimes they never actually committed. It is also estimated that as many as twenty-three innocent persons were executed in the United States between 1905 and 1974.

Evidence of wrongful executions is the reason Great Britain abolished the death penalty. The arrest, trial, and execution many years ago of Timothy Evans, who was accused of murder, was the catalyst for the shift away from the death penalty. After Evans was hanged, evidence revealed that his main accuser was actually the one who committed the murder.

If evidence of injustice has occurred in so-called progressive Western nations, with all the trappings of due process and human rights, then it stands to reason that such abuses could occur in a system less refined in such processes. We have seen that the Saudi culture is a conservative culture bound by religious tradition affecting political and social values, and of course the administration of justice. Saudi Arabia is an evolving nation in terms of social and political development. The discovery of oil spurted unprecedented growth focusing overnight international attention on the once-isolated desert nation. Although some criticize the document as non-substantive, the Kingdom has made some progress toward human rights by drafting a constitution in 1992.

The question remains: are the nurses guilty or innocent? The following pages present a summary of the evidence for and against them. To reach a decision on whether or not they are factually guilty, factually innocent, or legally innocent, is a personal decision. Yet, if a jury tried the murder case, would they be convicted? Is there reasonable doubt?

First, a word about evidence itself, of which there are several types. One type is direct evidence, as offered by an eyewitness to a crime, a videotape, or photo. This type of evidence is difficult to dispute assuming credibility of the witness and so forth. Another is real evidence such as a weapon or other physical items found at the scene. A common type of evidence is circumstantial evidence, which is presented when weapons, witnesses, or more tangible evidence are not found. Most cases are proven by circumstantial evidence. Circumstantial evidence is indirect evidence linking the accused to the crime. Offenders have been convicted of murder without discovering the victim's body, or finding a murder weapon. In other words, if enough pieces of the puzzle fit, all that is important is that the judge or jury believes beyond a reasonable doubt that the named person(s) committed the crime. In Western societies, a confession without supporting evidence is not sufficient to convict. Supporting evidence is any direct, real and circumstantial evidence that links the accused to a crime, such as finding the murder weapon on the accused and so forth.

The Factual Guilt Scenario

We know the nurses gave confessions admitting culpability to the murder of Yvonne Gilford. Deborah Parry is alleged to be the main attacker, with Lucille McLauchlan simply swept up as an accessory.

We also know they were held in custody for nearly 10 days without the benefit of counsel or diplomatic assistance. In due-process-oriented societies, a confession without other trustworthy evidence is insufficient to convict. Confessions taken under duress without the benefit of counsel are simply not admissible in Western societies. In theory, Sharia judges as well must be 100 percent convinced that the confessions are freely given.

So what is the case against the nurses absent the confessions? Were the Sharia judges presented with other evidence, as alleged throughout the trial? Evidence we know nothing about? However, we do not know, and probably will never know, but let's play judge for a moment. Let's examine what we do know, at least what has been revealed through various sources, and decide if the evidence is conclusive to convict.

The evidence against the nurses is circumstantial, since there are no eyewitnesses. The police did not offer any evidence (as far as we know) other than the confessions, although it was reported that they had "boxes of evidence" in the courtroom. A video of one of the nurses withdrawing funds with Gilford's bankcard was also mentioned, as was evidence that McLauchlan was caught by the bank manager using Gilford's bankcard after the murder. While these "smoking gun" allegations were mentioned by more than one authority close to the case, none of it was officially presented at trial.

As we have learned, confessional justice is the basis of conviction in Saudi Arabia. Circumstantial evidence absent a confession is inadmissible! However, circumstantial evidence may create the climate for the police to seek a confession. So evidently, the Saudi police had sufficient evidence to believe that McLauchlan and Parry killed Yvonne Gilford. We know the police interviewed a number of expatriates at the hospital before focusing on McLauchlan and Parry. Why?

Under the factual guilt scenario, the nurses went to Yvonne Gilford's apartment, either separately or together. While there, a dispute over sex or money broke out. Most likely it was a long-standing dispute between Yvonne Gilford and one or both of the convicted nurses.

In disputes such as this, there was probably no premeditated intentional design to kill Yvonne Gilford. The murder resulted after a heated dispute, suggesting a passion-oriented spontaneous killing. Some motives and "who done it" theories are discussed in Chapter four.

But to establish the culpability of McLauchlan and Parry, and to build a case against them, we need to prove such evidence as familiarity with the deceased and the accused. The credibility of the accused (are they trustworthy or not) is important, as is motive, statements of others who knew the deceased and accused, method of crime operation, and other physical indicators pointing to guilt.

Co-workers of Lucille McLauchlan and Deborah Parry indicated both were friends of Yvonne Gilford. The three were often seen together attending social functions, particularly the Delta club. This establishes a relationship and familiarity between the three. McLauchlan and Parry were among the last to see Yvonne Gilford alive. McLauchlan and other nurses visited Yvonne Gilford in her apartment on the night of the murder. McLauchlan admits the visit in her book.

McLauchlan acknowledges that she and Yvonne Gilford bought a bicycle together, suggesting an ongoing friendship between the two. There were statements by co-workers that a lesbian relationship was going on between Gilford and either McLauchlan or Parry.

But who was having the relationship? Maybe Deborah Parry was involved with Gilford, because Parry had no ongoing male relationships, whereas McLauchlan was engaged to be married. Having lost her loved ones, Parry may have been more susceptible to such a relationship due to a need for a caring companionship. Parry may have given in to Gilford's requests. And, there was information that Gilford was regarded as a lesbian by more than one co-worker at the compound. But again, this was speculation fueled by the police.

Other co-workers were aware of McLauchlan's past arrest record for theft in Scotland. She allegedly lied to get her job in Saudi Arabia, and continues to deny the theft despite her conviction. The method of stealing in Scotland (taking a patient's bankcard) is similar to her alleged crime in Saudi of taking Yvonne Gilford's bankcard and withdrawing from the ATM after her death. Is there a connection to her behavior, or is it mere coincidence? At the very least, this establishes a weakness in McLauchlan's character.

There was testimony by a long-term British hospital employee that Yvonne Gilford was a loanshark, tied to Filipino enforcers. This loan shark connection was mentioned by more than one former employee of the hospital. Maybe Parry or McLauchlan owed money to Gilford and refused to pay the debt. Information came forth that the three nurses were seen at a compound party a few days before the murder, quarreling. One expatriate states that Parry admitted to her that she (Parry) had an argument with Gilford weeks before the murder. Now we have familiarity with tension.

A co-worker testified that after the murder, Deborah Parry had numerous scratches over both her arms. Parry dismissed the injuries as cat scratches. The same co-worker testified that Parry knew about the detailed facts of the murder before anyone else did, and she was "acting strangely, as if she was being watched."

Parry's hairdresser stated that clumps of hair were missing from Parry's head after the murder. Lucille McLauchlan sent an unusual amount of money home after the murder, raising questions about the timing of such transactions. The police also stated that McLauchlan used Gilford's bankcard after the murder, and that she had an unusual amount of cash in her possession when arrested

Jon Ashbee, Deborah Parry's brother-in-law, who spent a great deal of time in Saudi Arabia visiting his sister in law and meeting with Saudi authorities, revealed that McLauchlan had telexed £3,005 back to Britain immediately after Gilford's death. The amount exceeded her monthly £980 salary. The money was not sent to her account, but to that of her fiancé, Grant Ferrie.

McLauchlan's reaction to the money transfers was that the money was from her stash fund. She had, she said, brought £2,200 out from Britain to Saudi Arabia for emergencies and was keen to send it back because she feared it would be stolen. When he asked her why her bank records did not show a withdrawal of £2,200 immediately prior to departure to Saudi, she reportedly stated that she had put a bit aside each month stashed in a "posy-hole" in her bedroom.

There is no evidence of an unlawful violent entry into Gilford's apartment, suggesting that the killer or killers either used a passkey, slipped into the apartment unnoticed, or were originally invited. McLauchlan admitted she had a key to Gilford's apartment. It was common practice for hospital workers to have keys to each other's apartments. No loud noises or screams were reported coming from Gilford's apartment.

The nurses indicated they were tortured and abused in police custody. Yet there was no physical evidence of such abuse. This hurts the credibility of the nurses, since they vehemently complain of such injuries during their detainment. The killing of Yvonne Gilford resembled a passion killing, resulting from a struggle. A knife was used and was the cause of death. Most likely two persons killed Yvonne Gilford, or at least one very strong person, due to the number of injuries. There are allegations by other expatriates that Yvonne Gilford was involved in a passionate relationship with Parry or McLauchlan.

Since their arrival home, both nurses have been "at each others' throats," blaming each other for their misfortune. McLauchlan, in her book, portrays herself as poor little victimized working class lass, who despite ill treatment at the hands of Saudi cops, held up under the strain of confinement to ultimately prevail through love and faith. Parry, on the other hand, is portrayed as a fragile, snobbish, drugged up manic depressive "bitch from hell!"

Although McLauchlan denies killing Gilford, her detailed accounts of her prison experiences and the events surrounding the murder are remarkable. However, she fails to offer any substantive explanation or theories as to whom may have killed Yvonne Gilford.

According to the autopsy report, the stabbing of Gilford was the cause of death. The stabbings were numerous and vicious, not controlled, suggesting a passion killing. The crime scene, with the exception of the bloodstains found on the bedroom floor, was virtually absent of evidence. Since the crime scene was clean, the killer(s) took time to remove or destroy evidence. This further suggests that the murderer(s) remained at the scene without fear of detection (familiarity with the apartment). This also suggests that the killers were meticulous and careful. Nurses are trained in detail.

What about evidence that blond hair was found clutched in Gilford's hand? First of all, the hair was reported to be an off color, which could have been light brown. Police sources indicated that the hair most likely belonged to Gilford herself.

The Factual Innocence Scenario:

Now let's summarize the evidence suggesting someone else may have committed the murder, and the nurses are factually innocent. The alleged murder weapon, a kitchen knife, had no traces of Gilford's blood. There were no eyewitnesses, nor anyone who saw placing either McLauchlan or Parry leaving Yvonne's apartment in the early morning hours. No physical evidence such as hair or fibers belonging to Gilford were found on the clothing of McLauchlan or Parry. No fingernail scrapings were taken from Yvonne Gilford. If any of this evidence was taken, it was never revealed at trial or publicly presented.

According to Parry, the reported scratches on her arms were the result of her cat, and the missing clumps of hair reported by her hairdresser resulted from a previous bad haircut. McLauchlan stated she received money from her parents, which would explain why she had extra funds. She also saved money in her room, and sent money home just prior to being arrested.

Other expatriates alleged Yvonne Gilford operated a loan sharking business and had many enemies. She reportedly used Filipino henchmen to collect her debts. Many expatriates knew that loan sharks known to be vicious roamed the Aramco Corporation. This information suggests that anyone with a grudge against Gilford could have killed her. Remember, a similar type of murder occurred at the compound a couple of years before the murder of Yvonne Gilford. In that case, a Filipino nurse was killed, but there was little publicity about the murder.

Yvonne Gilford complained to another expatriate that a security guard was stalking her. It was alleged that security guards operated a loan sharking and prostitution business at the compound. According to Parry, after the murder of Yvonne Gilford, five guards were arrested before the two Britons. Reports circulated around the compound that all were fired. Two ended up in hospital, and another disappeared. One officer is believed to be related to a member of the police team that obtained the nurses' confessions.

Lucille McLauchlan was engaged to get married. There was no evidence of lesbian relationships in either nurse's background. Although there were accusations, no one observed a lesbian relationship between the nurses. Even under Sharia law, accusations of sexual misconduct such as adultery requires witnesses. It was known that Yvonne Gilford reportedly left her bedroom window open on several occasions, with the air conditioning on. Her body was found on the bedroom floor, suggesting that the killer may have entered through the window.

The killing of Gilford had to be completed by someone who had the strength to control her. The wounds suggest that a struggle took place. How could a violent struggle take place so close to the security shack without anyone knowing or hearing anything? This adds credence to the theory that security was involved. Women were segregated in separate housing quarters (away from married employees and non-Westerners), and security was extremely tight in the compound, but security officers had open access to the compound.

What about the alleged clump of blond hair found in Yvonne Gilford's clutched hand? Both nurses are brunettes. A man's bracelet was found in Gilford's bedroom. It is known that other friends of Yvonne Gilford visited her the night before she was murdered, and it is alleged that Gilford was harassed by a male security guard.

As discussed, such groups as Amnesty International have criticized the Saudi government and police for human rights violations. There are reports that the Saudis resort to duress to get a confession. After their arrest, the nurses were in custody and questioned for nearly 10 days. They were denied visitations. What this suggests is that the nurses underwent exhaustive interrogations, which may cause anyone to say anything.

Lucille McLauchlan's book is full of detailed accounts of her life in prison. She denies she and Parry were involved with the murder. Are these determined, repetitious denials an indication that she is innocent? After all, neither McLauchlan nor Parry attempted to flee the country after the murder.

The way the police treated McLauchlan and Parry after their conviction is suspicious. McLauchlan was permitted to get married while in prison. The Saudis even provided a cake for the ceremony. Is this the way you treat a doomed person, someone who is factually guilty? Or is this a form of reconciliation; let's kiss and make up!

What about the behavior of the nurses after the murder? They did not act as if they were guilty, except that Parry was acting a bit odd, according to co-workers. Which raises another question. It is known that Parry was emotionally distraught after the murders, and she has a history of emotional problems resulting from previous family deaths. Given this information, is she capable of killing Gilford--or anyone else, for that matter? It was reported she didn't report to work for a couple of days after the murder. But for the most part, the two continued to work, shop at the mall, purchase clothing and makeup. Either they are cool customers or deceptive psychopaths.

The question we have to consider is sufficiency of evidence. Absent the confessions, which were reportedly examined by forensic experts and found to be faulty, is the evidence sufficient to convict the nurses? Do you feel enough evidence was established to reasonably conclude the nurses are guilty? Do you feel they are guilty by a preponderance of evidence, which means over 50 percent guilty? Do you feel they are guilty beyond a reasonable doubt, which does not mean absolute certainty, but close to it. Maybe one of the nurses is guiltier than the other. But who? Why?

Maybe the nurses are factually guilty. But what about the police investigation? Either the police believed they had the right culprits and confessions were all that was necessary, or they blundered big time! In the early stages of the investigation, the police appeared to pursue the right steps in the investigation. They interviewed prospective witnesses, collected evidence and so forth. But in a confessional justice system such as Saudi Arabia, focus is on the perpetrators, which brings us back to the importance of a confession, the system under which the police work.

Although many believe the nurses are guilty, there is no way to know what actually occurred in Yvonne Gilford's apartment. If there was other substantive evidence against the nurses, such as DNA, fingernail scrapings from Gilford, it wasn't presented. There are only the confessions, which were later retracted.

Out of this whole mess one fact is clear. Salah Al-Hejailan and his defense team exposed Saudi justice, or at least brought to the table certain questionable practices, which of course is their duty. The legal documents prepared by Hejailan attacking the case against the nurses are unequaled in Saudi Arabia criminal defense. Even Amnesty International, a constant critic of Saudi justice, spoke highly of Hejailan's precedent-setting work in the case.

"Of all other trials in Saudi Arabia, this one stands out," said Sharouf Al Ammry, of Amnesty International in London. *"The difference is that the defendants have been offered access to lawyers. This is unprecedented in the Saudi justice system. We welcome that very much. Maybe there is a change in the government's mind. It is not clear for us whether it will be a universal rule on all other trials in Saudi Arabia. If not...we will ask why."*

For the first time in the legal history of Saudi Arabia, the profile of the criminal defense attorney was raised one giant notch. But will all this lead to some sort of magical change in Saudi justice? Will we see more rights granted to criminal defendants? Probably not! Saudi Arabia is a deeply religious nation and, yes, there is evidence of human rights violations. By Western standards, women are treated unequally; yes, some laws are barbaric; and yes, criminal punishments are severe. But this is their system of justice. Anyone traveling to the Kingdom is informed of their customs, just as the nurses were advised when they joined the hospital staff in 1996. The Saudis do not promote tourism, nor do they crave publicity; and why should they care about what citizens from other nations feel in the first place?

Reports from expatriates and Saudi citizens who wish to remain anonymous, draconian laws, human rights violations, and abusive police practices permeate the Kingdom. But the Saudis are quick to point out that the violent crime rate is low (as compared to most other nations) and unfair laws and other questionable justice practices crop up in so-called progressive Western nations as well. Point well taken!

As long as violent crime remains a blip on the screen, a social aberration, nothing much will change. Why should it? Change will probably not occur unless there is a sudden surge of violent crime. But in spite of the problems and complaints of the Saudi system, we must recognize and respect the fact that their culture is incompatible with most Westerners. The Saudi system is a private system, not seeking political or social guidance from secular legalists or Western do-gooders.

Expatriates pursuing employment or travel within the Kingdom must understand the realty of their system or simply stay away (see Appendix E for travel advisory information on Saudi Arabia).

From a Westerner's perspective and probably a number of others, the nurses were denied due process. Whether the nurses killed Yvonne Gilford or not, they were detained an unusually long period of time. And, if you follow the complaints of the nurses, the police questioning and investigative process was appalling. Keep in mind these were Western expatriates. Imagine if the accused persons were from a Third World nation without benefit of counsel or media exposure. Sadly, we probably would never hear of the case.

Are the nurses guilty? While there are certainly enough theories, a number of facts that simply do not add up. When I first started writing, I of course interviewed some of the key lawyers in the case. Most notably, Salah Al-Hejailan, Michael Dark, and Rodger Pannone. I felt compelled to ask the question as to whether they believed the nurses were factually guilty. As expected I received answers ranging from "I don't know," or "we may never really know," to pregnant pauses followed by poignant criticisms of Saudi justice process, including the role of the police. We must remember that the Hejailan team devoted most of their work to the negotiation process after the nurses were convicted, not to the typical defense task of courtroom defense. But the evidence against the nurses was revealing. The alleged possession of Gilford's bankcard by McLauchlan, where she reportedly was caught using the card of a dead co-worker, after making several previous trips to the bank with the same card was suspicious. Also dubious was the money she transferred back to England on several occasions prior to her arrest. McLauchlan's behavior after the killing, such as washing her clothes shortly after the murder, raise serious questions. Parry also seemed particularly upset after the murder, which may not be unusual by itself, but considering she had scratches on her arm, and clumps of hair missing does pose additional questions. If the Saudi system allowed the admittance of circumstantial evidence, assuming such evidence existed and was properly gathered, there probably wouldn't be much debate.

Mick O'Connell, an Australian journalist who trotted around the kingdom investigating the case, and interviewing Hejailan, wrote an insightful book. The book titled Mercy, (Harper Collins 1999) is an investigative analysis of the facts surrounding the death of Yvonne Gilford. His conclusion, as is mine, is that the nurses are guilty of murdering Yvonne Gilford (I came to my conclusion before reading his book or McLauchlan's). There are too many facts that point in the direction that the nurses were culpable. Under Saudi jurisprudence, the nurses were legally tried and found guilty.

Although both nurses retracted their confessions, the evidence gathered by the police (although not publicly presented), was sufficient to pursue the confessions, which of course is necessary under their system. I do not agree with the confessional based system, the lengthy police questioning, or the way the courts kept the entire process secret; but as stated earlier, I accept it because it is their system! Naturally, a Western defense lawyer would have a field day with this case. After all, the presumption of innocence and preservation of due process is fundamental to achieve justice. In other words, in Western courts, the prosecution (state), has the burden of proof, which means all relevant evidence must be openly presented to allow cross examination, and a judge or jury to reach a verdict. But under Western justice, a convicted person in some cases, may have his or her sentence commuted by an executive official in the interest of justice. A governor of a state, or the president, for example, may reduce the sentence of death to life imprisonment. Under certain circumstances, they may pardon offenders. Under the Saudi system, the King pardoned the nurses in the interest of justice, or in the interest of the Saudi economy, as some would argue. In the end, some argue that justice was finally shown for the nurses, but was it really just for all?

ЄPILOGUЄ

The intent of this book is to provide an awareness of Islam and Saudi Arabian justice and culture within the framework of the Gilford murder case. It is also a quick overview of the Middle East, which continues to remain one of the worlds hot spots when it comes to political and religious battles. Fanning the flames of Middle East criticism are the terrorist acts of Iran, Iraq, and Libya, and the endless turmoil between Israel and the Palestinians. The 1993 New York City Trade Center bombings by Islamic militants, and more recently, the 1998 bombings of American embassy buildings in Kenya and Tanzania, are further reminders of Muslim militancy. Wealthy Saudi malcontent Osama Bin Laden was booted out of the Kingdom years ago (in 1999, Bin Laden made the Federal Bureau of Investigation top ten list for fugitives, with a $5 million bounty for anyone who can provide information leading to his arrest) for masterminding and funding these brutal and cowardly attacks. These are examples of Muslim militancy aimed at ousting Americans and other Western influences from Muslim countries, particularly Saudi Arabia.

In spite of the call for violence against Western nations by Muslim militants such as Bin Laden, and Mideast bully and billionaire to boot, Saddam Hussein, Islamic law as expressed in the Koran opposes all uses of force except in the case of war or punishment of criminals. Even in war the infliction of injury to women and children is forbidden, as is the use of force against innocent civilians. But, as with most law, there are those who interpret religious edicts to suit particular needs.

Thus many passages in the Koran as well as traditional teachings by Mohammed disapprove of violence aimed at the innocent. These teachings are contrary to the acts of Islamic terrorists who employ violence in the name of religion. We should not blame an entire religion for the explosive violence and flawed interpretations of a few criminals, just as we should not blame all right-to-life Christians for those few renegades who bomb abortion clinics. All religions and political groups have their share of self serving fanatics with so-called visions of morality and justice.

Setting aside isolated examples of actual terror, most of what the average person understands about Muslims results from distorted media accounts or twisted Hollywood films portraying Muslims as bearded religious fanatics, hijacking airplanes, bombing government buildings, and praising Allah. The fictional Hollywood production of The Siege, set in New York City and released in 1998, was one such film depicting Muslim terrorists bombing buildings and buses, killing innocent women and children. Obviously, the film does little to soften the image of Islamic people or the Muslim religion. These falsely malicious portrayals are damaging, resulting in negative labeling. Such perceptions are as absurd as characterizing all Christian fundamentalists as whiny, limp-wristed, Bible-thumpers, or all Catholic priests as sexually-repressed pedophiles pursuing naive altar boys.

We live in a world where people are prone to stereotyping a group by the actions of a few, resulting from ignorance fueled by prejudice or outside troublemakers. Political and religious fanatics unfortunately permeate all societies, but they are in the minority—albeit a dangerous one at that.

Regardless of religious teachings, family influences, and the law, Western nations are home to many hoodlums and political lamebrains. Such bloody outcasts are found in all colors, religions, and age groups. We read of white supremacists, often known as skinheads, viciously attacking immigrants and minorities, right-to-life Christians bombing abortion clinics, or violent street thugs killing each other over clothing color; these groups qualify as terrorists in any book.

The constant turmoil and killings in Northern Ireland, over religion and politics, have caused the needless deaths of many innocent persons, Protestants and Catholics alike. In the United States, the 1995 Oklahoma City bombing is a tragic warning of what depraved American right-wing fanatics are capable of achieving given a little fertilizer, combined with psychopathic personalities, and a mission of hate. So what does this have to do with the Gilford case or Saudi Arabian justice in general? I firmly believe all religions have redeeming qualities, bringing to the table certain values and beliefs we should embrace and cherish. And I can argue that some religious beliefs or messengers of the gospel have seriously undermined or violated human rights and freedoms in the name of religion. We have unfortunately seen this in history and we are seeing it today. In other words, you need not go far to find religious charlatans and false prophets, preaching one thing and practicing another.

It has been said that Islam is an imposing and virtuous religion, and some of its legal practices make moral sense. The Islamic faith is a practical, straightforward religion with supporters such as George Bernard Shaw, the late, famed Irish comic dramatist, literary critic, and winner of the Nobel Prize for Literature in 1925, who offered the following position:

"Islam is a religion without any mythology. Its teachings are simple and intelligible. It is free from superstitions and irrational beliefs. The oneness of God, the prophethood of Muhammad, and the concept of life after death are the basic articles of its faith. They are based on reason and sound logic. All of the teachings of Islam flow from those basic beliefs and are simple and straightforward. There is no hierarchy of priests, no far-fetched abstractions, no complicated rites and rituals."

However, secrecy invites criticism or at least suspicion, particularly when justice and human rights are in question. In Western society, we are not accustomed to private tribunals or denial of adversarial justice. But if we are to criticize or blame another system, we must understand why. There can be serious consequences for those who criticize a religious belief.

Salmon Rushdie's book *Satanic Verses*, which was published in 1988, chastised the Islamic religion, and didn't exactly forge him any friendships with Muslim clerics, particularly Shiite fundamentalists from Iran. Muslims strive toward the example of the Prophet Mohammed more than that of any other human; in defaming him, Rushdie attacked the very character of one billion Muslims. Rushdie's novel struck viciously "at the most basic principles" of Islamic belief. And the result for Rushdie was self-imposed exile.

In 1989, Ayatollah Ruhollah Khomeini, then Leader of the Islamic Republic of Iran, issued a fatwa (religious decree) declaring that the British author should be executed for having insulted Islam. Since then, and justifiably fearing for his life, the author has lived under constant police protection, and all his public appearances are undertaken amid tight security. Rushdie basically became a recluse in England after the death sentence was pronounced. However, in 1999, the decree calling for Rushdie's death ended, allowing the author to rejoin the human race.

It is now the fall of 1999 and the nurses have been home for well over a year. Executions continue in the Kingdom for murder, robbery and drug trafficking. Executions continue in the United States for intentional murder. The charismatic and energetic Tony Blair remains the British Prime Minister, and the aging King Fahad continues to rule the desert Kingdom despite reports of his declining health. The hardworking globetrotting Salah Al-Hejailan and his associates continue to engage in International legal work, although with less notoriety than found in the Gilford case.

As for Lucille McLauchlan, she never served a day of prison time for her theft conviction. Instead, she was given community service. Her name has been removed from the nursing register, and she is now starting a family. Deborah Parry is still working as a nurse in England and is unmarried. Frank Gilford did not respond to my request for an interview. I do not blame him; he has probably had enough publicity. Many of the other characters have gone their separate ways, leaving behind a case that brought international attention, and a partial unveiling of the conservative Saudi justice process. The Gilford murder did much to expose the Islamic justice process as applied in Saudi Arabia, by providing an understanding and appreciation of a system that for the most part has been mysterious and secretive.

Appendix A

Timeline of Key Events:

1996	May	Yvonne Gilford arrives in Saudi Arabia
1996	September	Lucille McLauchlan and Deborah Parry arrive in Saudi Arabia
1996	12 December	Yvonne Gilford found murdered in her apartment
1996	12-18 December	McLauchlan and Parry questioned about murder
1996	19 December	McLauchlan and Parry Arrested for the murder
1996	23 December	Both nurses write confessions
1996	25 December	Nurses make a Video Reenactment of crime
1996	28 December	First visit with the nurses by British Council
1997	4 January	Nurses first meeting with Hejailan defense lawyers
1997	13 January	First Hearing before the Sharia Court
1997	2 February	Yvonne Gilford buried in Australia
1997	10 March	Hejailan meets with British Ambassador about case
1997	29 March	Defense Rationale of Early Waiver of Death Penalty prepared by Hejailan and given to Frank Gilford

1997	2 April	Gilford turns down appeal to waive death penalty if nurses are found guilty of intentional murder
1997	19 May	Court trial begins: Nurses deny in open court killing Yvonne Gilford
1997	9 July	Court Hearing: Gilford family insists on death penalty
1997	20 July	Court Adjourned: Defense to obtains evidence Muriel Gilford, mother of deceased, is not a mentally competent heir
1997	3 September	Deborah Parry sentenced: Death by beheading (although unconfirmed)
1997	19 September	Frank Gilford signs deed of settlement for Blood money offer
1997	22 September	Nurses agree to blood money settlement
1997	23 September	Lucille McLauchlan convicted: Accessory to murder, sentenced to 800 lashes Parry's sentence has not been publicly announced
1997	24 September	Blood money offered to Frank Gilford
1997	15 October	Blood money accepted
1997	16 November	Death penalty formally waived by Frank Gilford
1997	30 November	Lucille McLauchlan marries Grant Ferrie in prison
1997	1 December	Attorney Salah Hejailan writes Genuine Commercial Grief Frank Gilford
1998	18 May	King Fahd pardons Deborah Parry and Lucille McLauchlan
1998	21 May	Both nurses return to the United Kingdom
1998	14 September	Deborah Parry returns to nursing in England
1998	November	The book Trial by Ordeal is published: Lucille McLauchlan's experiences in a Saudi prison.
1998	December	Lucille McLauchlan-Ferrie convicted: 1996 theft of 300 pounds from an elderly patient.
1999	July	The book Mercy is published: An Australian journalist's version of the case (recommended reading).

NOTE: Dates are approximate

Appendix B

Saudi Arabia—Constitution
{ Adopted on: March 1992 }
{Adopted by Royal decree of King Fahd }

Chapter 1 General Principles

Article 1
The Kingdom of Saudi Arabia is a sovereign Arab Islamic state with Islam as its religion; God's Book and the Sunnah of His Prophet, God's prayers and peace be upon him, are its constitution, Arabic is its language and Riyadh is its capital.

Article 2
The state's public holidays are Id al-Fitr and Id al-Adha. Its calendar is the Hegira calendar.

Article 3
The state's flag shall be as follows:
(a) It shall be green.
(b) Its width shall be equal to two-thirds of its length.
(c) The words "There is but one God and Mohammed is His Prophet" shall be inscribed in the center with a drawn sword under it. The statute shall define the rules pertaining to it.

Article 4

The state's emblem shall consist of two crossed swords with a palm tree in the upper space between them. The statute shall define the state's anthem and its medals.

Chapter 2 Monarchy

Article 5
(a) The system of government in the Kingdom of Saudi Arabia is that of a monarchy.
(b) Rule passes to the sons of the founding King, Abd al-Aziz Bin Abd al-Rahman al-Faysal Al Sa'ud, and to their children's children. The most upright among them is to receive allegiance in accordance with the principles of the Holy Koran and the Tradition of the Venerable Prophet.
(c) The King chooses the Heir Apparent and relieves him of his duties by Royal order.
(d) The Heir Apparent is to devote his time to his duties as an Heir Apparent and to whatever missions the King entrusts him with.
(e) The Heir Apparent takes over the powers of the King on the latter's death until the act of allegiance has been carried out.

Article 6

Citizens are to pay allegiance to the King in accordance with the holy Koran and the tradition of the Prophet, in submission and obedience, in times of ease and difficulty, fortune and adversity.

Article 7

Government in Saudi Arabia derives power from the Holy Koran and the Prophet's tradition.

Article 8 [Government Principles]

Government in the Kingdom of Saudi Arabia is based on the premise of justice, consultation, and equality in accordance with the Islamic Shari'ah.

Chapter 3 Features of the Saudi Family

Article 9

The family is the kernel of Saudi society, and its members shall be brought up on the basis of the Islamic faith, and loyalty and obedience to God, His Messenger, and to guardians; respect for and implementation of the law, and love of and pride in the homeland and its glorious history as the Islamic faith stipulates.

Article 10

The state will aspire to strengthen family ties, maintain its Arab and Islamic values and care for all its members, and to provide the right conditions for the growth of their resources and capabilities.

Article 11

Saudi society will be based on the principle of adherence to God's command, on mutual cooperation in good deeds and piety and mutual support and inseparability.

Article 12

The consolidation of national unity is a duty, and the state will prevent anything that may lead to disunity, sedition and separation.

Article 13

Education will aim at instilling the Islamic faith in the younger generation, providing its members with knowledge and skills and preparing them to become useful members in the building of their society, members who love their homeland and are proud of its history.

Chapter 4 Economic Principles

Article 14

All God's bestowed wealth, be it under the ground, on the surface or in national territorial waters, in the land or maritime domains under the state's control, are the property of the state as defined by law. The law defines means of exploiting, protecting, and developing such wealth in the interests of the state, its security and economy.

Article 15

No privilege is to be granted and no public resource is to be exploited without a law.

Article 16

Public money is sacrosanct. The state has an obligation to protect it and both citizens and residents are to safeguard it.

Article 17

Property, capital, and labor are essential elements in the Kingdom's economic and social being. They are personal rights which perform a social function in accordance with Islamic Shari'ah.

Article 18
The state protects freedom of private property and its sanctity. No one is to be stripped of his property except when it serves the public interest, in which case fair compensation is due.

Article 19
Public confiscation of money is prohibited and the penalty of private confiscation is to be imposed only by a legal order.

Article 20
Taxes and fees are to be imposed on a basis of justice and only when the need for them arises. Imposition, amendment, revocation and exemption is only permitted by law.

Article 21
Alms tax is to be levied and paid to legitimate recipients.

Article 22
Economic and social development is to be achieved according to a just and scientific plan.

Chapter 5 Rights and Duties

Article 23 [Islam]
The state protects Islam; it implements its Shari'ah; it orders people to do right and shun evil; it fulfills the duty regarding God's call.

Article 24 [Holy Places]
The state works to construct and serve the Holy Places; it provides security and care for those who come to perform the pilgrimage and minor pilgrimage through the provision of facilities and peace.

Article 25 [World Peace]
The state strives for the achievement of the hopes of the Arab and Islamic nation for solidarity and unity of word, and to consolidate its relations with friendly states.

Article 26 [Human Rights]
The state protects human rights in accordance with the Islamic Shari'ah.

Article 27 [Welfare Rights]
The state guarantees the rights of the citizen and his family in cases

of emergency, illness and disability, and in old age; it supports the system of social security and encourages institutions and individuals to contribute in acts of charity.

Article 28 [Work]
The state provides job opportunities for whoever is capable of working; it enacts laws that protect the employee and employer.

Article 29 [Science, Culture]
The state safeguards science, literature and culture; it encourages scientific research; it protects the Islamic and Arab heritage and contributes toward the Arab, Islamic and human civilization.

Article 30 [Education]
The state provides public education and pledges to combat illiteracy.

Article 31 [Health Care]
The state takes care of health issues and provides health care for each citizen.

Article 32 [Environment, Nature]
The state works for the preservation, protection, and improvement of the environment, and for the prevention of pollution.

Article 33 [Armed Forces]
The state establishes and equips the Armed Forces for the defense of the Islamic religion, the Two Holy Places, society, and the citizen.

Article 34 [Military Service]
The defense of the Islamic religion, society, and country is a duty or each citizen. The regime establishes the provisions of military service.

Article 35 [Citizenship]
The statutes define the Regulations governing Saudi Arabian nationality.

Article 36 [Arrest]
The state provides security for all its citizens and all residents within its territory and no one shall be arrested, imprisoned, or have their actions restricted except in cases specified by statutes.

Article 37 [Home]
The home is sacrosanct and shall not be entered without the permission of the owner or be searched except in cases specified by statutes.

Article 38 [Punishment, nulla poena]

Penalties shall be personal and there shall be no crime or penalty except in accordance with the Shari'ah or organizational law. There shall be no punishment except for acts committed subsequent to the coming into force of the organizational law.

Article 39 [Expression]

Information, publication, and all other media shall employ courteous language and the state's regulations, and they shall contribute to the education of the nation and the bolstering of its unity. All acts that foster sedition or division or harm the state's security and its public relations or detract from man's dignity and rights shall be prohibited. The statutes shall define all that.

Article 40 [Communication]

Telegraphic, postal, telephone, and other means of communications shall be safeguarded. They cannot be confiscated, delayed, read or listened to except in cases defined by statutes.

Article 41 [Residents' Duties]

Residents of the Kingdom of Saudi Arabia shall abide by its laws and shall observe the values of Saudi society and respect its traditions and feelings.

Article 42 [Asylum, Extradition]

The state shall grant the right to political asylum when the public interest demands this. Statutes and international agreements shall define the rules and procedures governing the extradition of common criminals.

Article 43 [Royal Courts]

The King's Court and that of the Crown Prince shall be open to all citizens and to anyone who has a complaint or a plea against an injustice. Every individual shall have a right to address the public authorities in all matters affecting him.

Chapter 6 The Authorities of the State

Article 44

The authorities of the state consist of the following: the judicial authority; the executive authority; the regulatory authority. These authorities cooperate with each other in the performance of their duties, in accordance with this and other laws. The King shall be the point of reference for all these authorities.

Article 45

The source of the deliverance of fatwa in the Kingdom of Saudi Arabia are God's Book and the Sunnah of His Messenger. The law will define the composition of the senior ulema body, the administration of scientific research, deliverance of fatwa and its (the body of senior ulema's) functions.

Article 46

The judiciary is an independent authority. There is no control over judges in the dispensation of their judgments except in the case of the Islamic Shari'ah.

Article 47

The right to litigation is guaranteed to citizens and residents of the Kingdom on an equal basis. The law defines the required procedures for this.

Article 48

The courts will apply the rules of the Islamic Shari'ah in the cases that are brought before them, in accordance with what is indicated in the Book and the Sunnah, and statutes decreed by the Ruler which do not contradict the Book or the Sunnah.

Article 49

Observing what is stated in Article 53, the courts shall arbitrate in all disputes and crimes.

Article 50

The King, or whoever deputizes for him, is responsible for the implementation of judicial rulings.

Article 51

The authorities establish the formation of the Higher Council of Justice and its prerogatives; they also establish the seniority of the courts and their prerogatives.

Article 52

The appointment of judges and the termination of their duties is carried out by Royal decree by a proposal from the Higher Council of Justice in accordance with the provisions of the law.

Article 53

The law establishes the seniority of the tribunal of complaints and its prerogatives.

Article 54
The law establishes the relationship between the investigative body and the Prosecutor-general, and their organization and prerogatives.

Article 55
The King carries out the policy of the nation, a legitimate policy in accordance with the provisions of Islam; the King oversees the implementation of the Islamic Shari'ah, the system of government, the state's general policies; and the protection and defense of the country.

Article 56
The King is the head of the Council of Ministers; he is assisted in carrying out his duties by members of the Council of Ministers, in accordance with the provisions of this and other laws. The Council of Ministers establishes the prerogatives of the Council regarding internal and external affairs, the organization of and co-ordination between government bodies. It also establishes requirements to be fulfilled by ministers, their prerogatives, the manner of their questioning and all issues concerning them. The law on the Council of Ministers and its prerogatives is to be amended in accordance with this law.

Article 57
(a) The King appoints and relieves deputies of the prime minister and ministers and members of the Council of Ministers by Royal decree.
(b) The deputies of the prime minister and ministers of the Council of Ministers are responsible, by expressing solidarity before the King, for implementing the Islamic Shari'ah and the state's general policy.
(c) The King has the right to dissolve and reorganize the Council of Ministers.

Article 58
The King appoints those who enjoy the rank of ministers, deputy ministers and those of higher rank, and relieves them of their posts by Royal decree in accordance with the explanations included in the law. Ministers and heads of independent departments are responsible before the prime minister for the ministries and departments which they supervise.

Article 59
The law defines the rules of the civil service, including salaries, awards, compensations, favors and pensions.

Article 60

The King is the commander-in-chief of all the armed forces. He appoints officers and puts an end to their duties in accordance with the law.

Article 61

The King declares a state of emergency, general mobilization and war, and the law defines the rules for this.

Article 62

If there is a danger threatening the safety of the Kingdom or its territorial integrity, or the security of its people and its interests, or which impedes the functioning of the state institutions, the King may take urgent measures in order to deal with this danger. And if the King considers that these measures should continue, he may then implement the necessary regulations to this end.

Article 63

The King receives Kings and Heads of State. He appoints his representatives to states, and he receives the credentials of state representatives accredited to him.

Article 64

The King awards medals, as defined by regulations.

Article 65

The King may delegate prerogatives to the Crown Prince by Royal decree.

Article 66

In the event of his traveling abroad, the King issues a Royal decree delegating to the Crown Prince the management of the affairs of state and looking after the interests of the people, as defined by the Royal decree.

Article 67

The regulatory authority lays down regulations and motions to meet the interests of the state or remove what is bad in its affairs, in accordance with the Islamic Shari'ah. This authority exercises its functions in accordance with this law and the laws pertaining to the Council of Ministers and the Consultative Council.

Article 68 [Consultative Council]

A Consultative Council is to be created. Its statute will specify how it is formed, how it exercises its powers and how its members are selected.

Article 69

The King has the right to convene the Consultative Council and the Council of Ministers for a joint meeting and to invite whomever he wishes to attend that meeting to discuss whatever matters he wishes.

Article 70

International treaties, agreements, regulations and concessions are approved and amended by Royal decree.

Article 71

Statutes are to be published in the Official Gazette and take effect from the date of publication unless another date is specified.

Chapter 7 Financial Affairs

Article 72

(a) The statute explains the provisions concerning the state's revenue and its entry in the state's general budget.
(b) Revenue is entered and spent in accordance with the rules specified in the statute.

Article 73

Any undertaking to pay a sum of money from the general budget must be made in accordance with the provisions of the budget. If it is not possible to do so in accordance with the provisions of the budget, then it must be done in accordance with Royal decree.

Article 74

The sale, renting or use of state assets is not permitted except in accordance with the statute.

Article 75

The statutes will define the monetary and banking provisions, the standards, weights and measures.

Article 76

The law will fix the state's financial year and will announce the budget by way of a Royal decree. It will also assess the revenues and expenditure of that year at least one month before the start of the financial year. If, for essential reasons, the budget is not announced and the new financial year starts, the budget of the previous year will remain in force until the new budget is announced.

Article 77

The competent body will prepare the state's final statement of account for the passing year and will submit it to the head of the council of ministers.

Article 78

The same provisions will apply both to the budgets of the corporate bodies and their final statements of account and to the state's budget and its final statement of account.

Chapter 8 Control Bodies

Article 79

All the state's revenues and expenditures will come under subsequent control and all the state's movable and immovable funds will be controlled in order to confirm the good use of these funds and their preservation. An annual report will be submitted on this matter to the head of the Council of Ministers. The law will define the competent control body and its obligations and prerogatives.

Article 80

Government bodies will come under control in order to confirm the good performance of the administration and the implementation of the statutes. Financial and administrative offenses will be investigated and an annual report will be submitted on this matter to the head of the Council of Ministers. The law will define the competent body in charge of this and it's obligations and prerogatives.

Chapter 9 General Provisions

Article 81

The implementation of this law will not prejudice the treaties and agreements signed by the Kingdom of Saudi Arabia with international bodies and organizations.

Article 82

Without violating the content of Article 7, no provision of this law whatsoever may be suspended unless it is temporary such as in a time of war or during the declaration of a state of emergency. This temporary suspension will be in accordance with the terms of the law.

Article 83

This law may only be amended in the same way as it was promulgated.

APPENDIX C

Rationale for Early Waiver of the Death Penalty
by Salah Hejailan March 27, 1997

The Saudi Arabian authorities investigating the death of Nurse Yvonne Gilford have make available to us a number of essential elements of their official report, in which they accuse two fellow Nurses Lucille McLauchlan and Deborah Parry of murder. In reaching this conclusion, the Saudi Arabian authorities depend not only on the confessions, since withdrawn, of Ms. McLauchlan and Ms. Parry, but also reportedly on physical evidence from the crime scene and on evidence that Ms. McLauchlan and Ms. Parry used the victim's ATM card after her death to withdraw money from her bank account.

We represent the accused Ms. McLauchlan and Ms. Parry in Saudi Arabia, together with the opportunity of obtaining assistance from criminal defense counsel in the United Kingdom.

There are several unique features and juxtapositions in this case that underlie the appeal for an early waiver of the death penalty by the family of the victim:

- These events are unprecedented for the Saudi Arabian judicial system in that only women are involved in the crime as victim and accused. That the women have all made a career of a most compassionate profession. That the crime is murder. That the women are all foreigners thousand of miles from home. That the foreigners are all Western. That legal counsel for the accused is being allowed to participate, indeed advocate in the proceedings.

- Justice in Saudi Arabia is based on Islamic law as applied in an Islamic community, and differs in a fundamental respect from Western justice in that in Saudi Arabia the fate of a person convicted of murder is left almost totally in the hands of the victim's immediate family. Such a decisive role for private individuals in the penal system is not recognized in the West.
- Neither Australia, where the victim's family lives, nor the United Kingdom, where the accused lived before their assignments in Saudi Arabia, had the death penalty. This unfortunate case has the potential for bringing about a clash of cultures across continents, when those adhering to the definition of values prevailing in Australia and the United Kingdom are put in the position of having to transfer and apply that set of values meaningfully within a foreign culture and within the deeply religious framework of Islam.
- Much will turn in this case, as in the prosecution of crimes generally in Saudi Arabia, on the confessions of the accused. In the West, a confession given in the course of an investigation must be rigorously examined and is now not alone determinative as to guilt. In Saudi Arabia, it will not however be an easy task to challenge written confessions pronounced in court before a judge, even if they have afterwards been withdrawn or exist in variant versions, and irrespective of the circumstances under which the confessions were given. The existence of even such confessions will also put a limit on the overall examination before the court of other evidence of the crime, and may very well have influenced the gathering of evidence at a certain point in the investigation.
- Our clients, Ms. McLauchlan and Ms. Parry, have since withdrawn their confessions, given in the days following their arrests without the benefit of counsel and without access to British diplomatic staff, on the basis that the confessions were extracted under duress. Our clients deny using Ms. Gilford's ATM card. In essence, our clients maintain that they did not kill Ms. Gilford and know nothing about the events surrounding Ms. Gilford's death, but it is the position of the Saudi Arabian authorities that, applying Islamic principles of proof, more than adequate evidence has been collected to the contrary.

Meanwhile the international media swirl with rumors and second-hand "facts," some tending to exonerate, others to implicate our clients, others broadening the field of suspects. Our investigation continues, including our effort to persuade the authorities to further review the official investigation and to reconsider the official report. Realistically, however, despite some alternative allegations or leads supported by written statements which appear to be credible, no coherent alternative theory has yet emerged for consideration by the police to account for Ms. Gilford's death that might lead the Saudi Arabian authorities to drop the charges against Ms. McLauchlan and Ms. Parry.

Please keep in mind that the Islamic jurisprudence of Saudi Arabia recognizes the fallibility of all human efforts to capture the truth. As such, even an authoritative report of this crime is not measured by exactly the same Western standard of proof "beyond a reasonable doubt." Instead, the authorities strive to reconstruct what probably happened, with all the limitations of human reason, and to reduce doubt, but they do not rule out the possibility of error. What takes place in this process is a good faith effort to solve the puzzle and to tell a story that accounts for the greatest number of the core facts.

The corollary of this different but no less valid way to pursue justice is that in a capital case, the Saudi Arabian court, having pronounced a guilty verdict on the basis of the official report, would not apply the death penalty if the immediate family of the victim permits the court to temper justice with mercy by waiving the family's right to demand the death of the accused. Absent that demand, punishment still attaches for the crime but takes the form of a prison sentence.

And so, the matter truly rests with the victim's brother, Mr. Frank Gilford, and his elderly mother living in Australia, who we understand are the only surviving members of Yvonne Gilford's immediate family. If the family's decision were to insist on the death penalty, that decision must be unanimous and must be pronounced formally and unequivocally before the Saudi Arabian judge who will seek to verify the seriousness and validity of their intention. Mr. Gilford should be aware that the family's demand for the death penalty would normally be accompanied by his own or his appointee's personally being present at the beheadings which would be carried out in public. We recognize of course that this entails a heavy responsibility on the Gilford family.

We submit that, based on the Gilfords' waiving the death penalty, further developments leading up to the formal trial and sentencing of Ms. McLauchlan and Ms. Parry can occur in a freer atmosphere which is more conducive towards reaching the Gilfords' ultimate goal of understanding what really took place on the night of Ms. Gilford's death. Out of the media glare over potential beheading, the relaxation might permit a more satisfactory reconstruction of the events surrounding Ms. Gilford's death. There may be extenuating circumstances that have no chance of being fully discussed with the death penalty impending.

Moreover, we can well imagine the Gilfords' dedicating the blood money discussed below, as well as other voluntary contributions, which may realistically be expected from those in Saudi Arabia, Australia, the

United Kingdom or persons elsewhere sympathetic to Ms. Gilford's memory, to some charitable effort or fund in furtherance of the benevolent actions of Ms. Gilford during her life. We note her philanthropy which has taken the form of her contributing to the education of poor and disadvantaged children.

There are also some opportunities for reform which could be explored in Ms. Gilford's memory if the atmosphere were less charged and more caring and cooperative. There are real issues of common interest, which we think would have been of concern to Ms. Gilford herself, including the welfare of nurses working in Saudi Arabia, investigation techniques in Saudi Arabia, attention to the mental health of one's co-workers, closer ties and support with family members working abroad, reducing the high stress level associated with the nursing profession, punishment versus treatment for crimes resulting from mental or stress disorders, and so forth.

We ask the Gilfords therefore to decide dispassionately, as hard as that may be, in a way that contributes to the memory of Ms. Gilford for the positive acts of kindness she performed.

We offer a short summary of the operation of the Islamic concept of Kisas, which underlies the possible imposition of the death penalty in the event of murder. Kisas under Islamic law is a punishment based on reciprocity, such that the punishment should be proportionate to the wrongful act. It should not be excessive. In a murder case with manifest intention to kill, Kisas is the death penalty. The punishment of Kisas is a deterrent punishment. It is intended to protect life and to establish the rule of law and thereby peace and order within a society.

However, under the rules of Islam as derived from the Koran and the Sunnah, the heirs of the deceased may elect to waive their right to Kisas and instead claim Diyah, that is blood money, which must be paid to them in full and without any unnecessary delay. Furthermore, the heirs of the deceased may come to a compromise with the guilty person and the terms of this compromise could be more favorable to the heirs than the literal application of Diyah. They may also decline to exercise any of the vested rights. If, as an important element of Kisas, the family of the victim waives the death penalty in return for Diyah or otherwise, there still attaches punishment but in accordance with the system of State-imposed prison sentences.

It is a recognized practice in Islam and in fact a requirement that goes without saying that contact with a victim's family, who may eventually control the fate of the accused, is to be established immediately upon the charging of the accused by the authorities. The conduct of the practice of Kisas is to be made sometime long before the trial and without any link to the precondition that the accused has already been convicted. This

helps in healing the wounds. It eases the mental pressure on all concerned. It may also encourage the authorities and others to search for the
truth in a less tense atmosphere.

We understand that some outside observers consider the practice of
seeking clemency from the victim's family before the trial to be a "high
risk strategy" in that it could be misunderstood, so they say, as a pre-judg-
ment of guilt, but in reality and in the Islamic context there is nothing
daring or risky about an early approach to the victim's family. On the
contrary, it is the culturally accepted way of dealing with and properly
channeling otherwise uncontrollable emotions in the aftermath of an
alleged murder.

The process is usually conducted on a wide scope with participation
by mature figures in both families, the victim's and the accuser's, and is
often done through spokesmen for the families. Although Kisas is triggered by individualistic announcement on the part of immediate family
members, it is actually meant to be a restraint on the attitude of the society to which those individuals belong. Kisas is meant to be a reflection
of the attitude and conscience of those individuals, and of the society.
Kisas requires that all family members should agree to the conclusion,
and abstention of one member would nullify the entire request for Kisas.
If among the heirs there is a child, then the request for Kisas must be
delayed until he becomes of age.

The reason in the case before us for making an appeal in writing to
be submitted to the victim's family is to help them in rationalizing their
position and to discourage individualistic or subjective intervention otherwise.

Perhaps this is an occasion for the West to realize the wisdom of the
Islamic rule of leaving the matter very much in the hands of the victim's
family, with some qualifications of course. This religious rule has a deep
and balanced foundation that may also enhance the role for the society
to intervene through its creditable members to mediate or conciliate and
to heal the wounds.

In contrast to this Islamic concept of Kisas which forms part of the
fabric of Islamic culture and which tempers the death penalty with the
predominant goal of making peace between the concerned families,
there stands the now centuries-long process in Western culture towards
abolition of the death penalty.

In such unique and novel circumstances, we call upon the Gilfords,
in keeping with the best values and traditions of our respective religions
and cultures to follow the lead of the Saudi Arabian approach to such a
case, which inclines towards mercy and forgiveness, and together with
which they can in their decision-making build on the great Western tradition regarding the death penalty which we have sketched above.

We repeat that we make this appeal before our clients may be found guilty of the crime for which they are accused. They protest their innocence, even in the face of the official report. We ask the Gilfords, however, to take account of the swiftness with which justice is meted out in Saudi Arabia and the evidentiary weight which normally attaches to such an official report as shall be issued in this case.

In acknowledgment of the grief which the Gilfords are suffering as well as the anxiety which the families of the accused are suffering and the potential conflict of ideas and traditions in this case, I would personally consider it my duty to extend an invitation and to cover the cost for Mr. Gilford to come to Saudi Arabia in order to acquaint himself with the circumstances in which his sister was living and perhaps to meet some of the judicial personalities in this country who would confirm to him the ideas set forth in this Rationale.

The time for the Gilfords' decision is ripe. The facts before them now will probably not change very much as time passes. The principles, which we ask them to rely on in making their decision, can be applied now, even on the imperfect record before them. Most importantly, by acting now to waive the death penalty, the Gilfords will be acting most effectively and in a timely manner to guide this terrible event to a close that issues from the nobler human impulses as befit Yvonne Gilford's memory.

APPENDIX D

Letter written to attorneys Rodger Pannone and
Peter Watson by Salah Hejailan.

March 13, 1997

Rodger Pannone, Esq.
Pannone & Partners
Manchester, England

Peter Watson, Esq.
Levy & McRae
Glasgow, Scotland

Re: Defense of Lucille McLauchlan and Deborah Parry

Gentlemen:
*I was surprised to receive Rodger Pannone's letter dated 7 March
1997, and then Peter Watson's letter dated 11 March 1997 and then yet
another letter from Mr. Pannone of the same date, which I did not appre-
ciate at all. I must now, as a distraction from addressing the merits of the
defense of Lucille McLauchlan and Deborah Parry, set the record straight
with you gentlemen, hoping that you will, on mature reflection and in the
best interests of our clients, retract the remarks that you have made in
these letters.*

*Let me make clear at the outset that I do not believe it is in the best
interests of our clients that you have created a situation where we are*

expending our respective debaters' skills in exchanging such notes among us. We have had extensive oral discussion of these same points, and I have as well spoken at length with the British Ambassador to Saudi Arabia, but you have expressly insisted on and provoked a written exchange. Indeed. I have traveled to England among other reasons to consult with you in person. Rodger Pannone was available; Peter Watson was not. Neither of you has as yet traveled to Saudi Arabia to meet me or to meet the nurses. There are numerous errors of fact in your series of letters, which I consider to be overwhelmingly self-serving, as I shall demonstrate below.

Secondly, it is about time for you to recognize that my law firm and I have, on a complimentary basis, been assisting and when necessary defending British citizens in this country for almost twenty years now, in view of our relationship with the Embassy and also to help establish precedents that will be useful in the interest of expatriates in Saudi Arabia, including the right to use lawyers in times of difficulty.

My law firm and I have incurred a great deal of expense over the years in such direction and we have been very pleased with the recognition and statements of gratitude issued by those individuals. You will not be surprised therefore to find me somewhat puzzled at what I have heard from you through Michael Dark about your expectation to recover expenses and develop funds for the defense of the nurses. The correspondence reveals that you gentlemen are terribly concerned about your covering the expenses of this representation. I must view your recent over-heated comments leading possibly to a diminution of your roles in these proceedings in the light of that obvious concern of yours. In short, I cannot take your remarks at face value.

Thirdly, you did not, as Mr. Pannone states in his 7 March letter, accept my invitation to be my U.K. agents in this case. In fact, on the contrary, you asked to be appointed my agents for your own reasons which I did not probe at the time.

Fourthly, I have not accepted, as Mr. Pannone states in his 7 March letter, that you "have already done far more that was expected" of you. You refer somewhat patronizingly to a lack of experience in Saudi Arabia in matters forensic. In the area in which we have called upon your expertise that is the examination of evidence, almost everything remains to be done. I look forward to your input—yet to come.

Fifthly, as regards my professional obligation to discuss the proposal concerning Mr. Gilford with my clients, please be assured that I am well aware of the necessity and advisability of doing so, and have taken care of that aspect of the question in cooperation with the British Embassy.

To the substance then of your series of letters:
  * *I have very carefully observed the rules of communication among professionals in circulating the draft text of the Appeal to be made*

to Mr. Gilford. I had from my part confined the document at the time in question between my office and you gentlemen. I had not yet provided the British Embassy with a copy. To my dismay, which I have bluntly brought to your attention during our telephone conference on 4 March from my hotel in London, I learned that, a few hours after handing over this document to Mr. Pannone late on the night of Monday, 3 March, he sent a copy in record time to the British Foreign Office which subsequently faxed a further copy to the British Embassy in Riyadh. Within an hour, that is early Tuesday morning 4 March, I received a call from the British Ambassador about this issue.

The document was in draft form and I was hoping to benefit from your inputs and to discuss the draft with you after you had reviewed it. Indeed, shortly afterwards the "Appeal" was re-titled "Rationale for Early Waiver of the Death Penalty," It was re-drafted in the third-person. There were other changes and the document continues to be revised. I had repeatedly stated to both of you to keep this document among us, until we had all discussed its contents, rationale and timing of release. It is untrue that, when I confronted you about your premature circulation in our phone conference on 4 March, I ever "accepted it was right and proper for (Mr. Pannone) to seek their views," meaning the views of the British Foreign Office on the 3 March draft of the Appeal. Moreover, I still do not know who else Mr. Pannone, without my knowledge, displayed this early draft to, whom he calls in his 7 March letter: "a number of informed individuals".

- *I received the British Ambassador at my residence in Riyadh on Monday evening, 10 March. The Ambassador asked me to delay release of the Rationale for a week or ten days, within which we would be receiving a report from the Jones Day lawyer, Mr. Phipps, who had gone to Australia to meet with the Gilfords. Perhaps the final form of the Rationale would be adjusted to reflect any outcome of that meeting. The substance would remain the same. The Ambassador appeared to be convinced of my strategy in principle and had no objection to it.*

- *I have told you repeatedly why prompting an early statement from Mr. Gilford would be appropriate and useful to us. There are reasons given in the text of the Rationale. Beyond that, I have told you and the Ambassador the other reasons for such a tactic at this stage, which I hope you will find convincing. I would like you to know that the reaction to my advocacy in Saudi Arabia will be greatly influenced by an early declaration from Mr. Gilford. If such declaration is positive, and he extends early clemency to take effect in the event of conviction, then it would naturally and unques-*

*tionably be useful for our defense. If Mr. Gilford's response is nega-
tive, it will still be useful because the pertinent authorities would
then see that the Australian family had elected to act in a way that
is not consistent with the prevailing values and laws of the U.K. or
Australia and are perhaps seeking unnecessary politicization of the
case. That will have a consequence favorable to our clients.*

- *Timing release of the Appeal/Rationale in relation to the visit of Mr.
Phipps with Mr. Gilford is a detail. It should hardly have engen-
dered a response of the magnitude of your series of letters. It would
seem that floating the trial balloon about the Rationale has accel-
erated Mr. Phipps' trip. So much the better. Indeed, the reaction in
the British and Australian press to my interviews in early March
has been positive and has laid a good foundation for release of the
actual text of the Rationale. You may not have seen these reports
carried around 10 and 11 March before writing your letters on 11
March. The reports carried in the Australian press do not, however,
indicate that there has been any recent softening in Mr. Gilford's
views regarding the death penalty.*

- *Perhaps one of you has spoken to Mr. Phipps, in which case I would
expect a briefing. I do not know on what basis you have been
"building a profile of Mr. Gilford, who appears to be a totally honest and reasonable individual." Perhaps you would share this valuable intelligence with me, as it does not conform with the portrait
of Mr. Gilford to be derived from his public statements. If Mr.
Gilford is as intellectually honest as you say, there should be no
problem in asking him to deal, with the assistance of knowledgeable counselors, with the Rationale supporting the action which we
are asking him to take. The Rationale has been re-drafted in the
third-person, so that a public discussion of these important issues
could be illuminating for Mr. Gilford. It is not meant at all to crush
him or inflame him. The Rationale is a considerate and compassionate document. The Rationale would not be served without
warning. Any so-called inflammatory wording could be toned
down, and has already been, but I do not agree with your list of
such phrases which are quoted out of context.*

*I would like you to know the law firm Jones Day are not a group of
priests or relaxation therapists. They are deemed to be among the most
aggressive litigators in the U.S. and they are not known at all for conciliation or clemency arrangements. Their involvement makes me even more
suspicious about the intention of the Gilford family to complicate this matter and raise its profile.*

*I do not agree that the Rationale should only be delivered in oral form,
although an appropriate person, whom you seem to think is Mr. Phipps,*

may spend time reviewing the matter with Mr. Gilford in person. With all due respect, left to the privacy of his own thoughts, Mr. Gilford has not taken the proper course from the perspective of our clients, and some gentile persuasion is appropriate.

- *Contrary to the patronizing remark in Mr. Pannone's letter dated 11 March, I have now had a great deal of opportunity to explain my position regarding the Appeal/Rationale to you and to the British Embassy. We maintain appropriate contact with the British Embassy in Riyadh and the British Consulate in Dammam, but Mr. Watson seems from his letter dated 11 March to have a rather colonialist view of the role of the British Foreign Office, with which I have no direct contact, as regards my legal representation as a Saudi Arabian Lawyer.*
- *Your reference to my having arranged an interview with BBC TV is totally wrong. We are harassed by news people all the time and we have acted very intelligently in communication with them, again in the best interests of the clients. This case has captured the media's attention well before my intervention or yours. It is not true that we have made an undertaking with you that any press statement will have to be notified through you to the McLauchlans and Ashbees in advance. But have undertaken to make best efforts to alert you and will continue to do so as a matter of professional courtesy.*

The meeting with BBC TV, at their own solicitation and at my hotel, was made on the occasion of the visit of Jonathan and Sandra Ashbee, your clients. They have been interviewed also, as you knew they would be, and I have saluted them for their proper handling. They seemed to be content and happy with what has been said.

Prior to that meeting. I had through Mr. Dark and Mr. Watson also invited the McLauchlan family to come and meet with me in London but, because of the distance, they have declined. Again, Mr. Watson was quite busy in court sessions, which I fully understand.

You both knew full well of my intention to approach Mr. Gilford in some manner in the coming period. I do not accept that my mentioning same to the BBC in general terms should have come as a surprise to either of you or to your clients (unless you had failed to inform them). Contrary to the statement of Mr. Pannone in his 11 March letter, I had no agreement with you that I will not approach Mr. Gilford. Quite the contrary, I have agreed with the British Ambassador to do just that.

I never said that I would refrain in the BBC interview from saying that we would be making an appeal or would be submitting a rationale to Mr. Gilford for his consideration. Sooner rather than later is correct. Did you think that I was only going to sit like a store mannequin to be photographed by a news organization?

What is this ominous reference in Mr. Pannone's 11 March letter to his obtaining a transcript of the BBC interview? If he now has it, let me see it.

Mr. Pannone also refers to certain "distressing" discussions I supposedly had with Mr. Ashbee over dinner. Whatever is Mr. Pannone referring to?

Mr. Pannone also says that I advised Mr. Ashbee and the McLauchlans to act in a way "inconsistent" with your relationship to them. What is Mr. Pannone talking about?

Mr. Pannone also states that I was speaking to the BBC contrary to the advice of lawyers in my office. What is he talking about?

This is a steady stream of unsubstantiated and snide insinuations that I will not tolerate.

I have in fact referred to both of you estimable gentlemen as my honorable colleagues whom I was coming to London to visit. I repeated words to that effect several times during the interview and at the subsequent dinner. If that portion was not aired, I do not think you should be distressed. Perhaps the media is creating friction, knowing the egos involved.

How then do we explain publicity why we are releasing now the full text of the Rationale for Early Waiver of the Death Penalty?

Justice is swift in Saudi Arabia. Although we hope to be given some opportunity to examine the evidence against the nurses, the opportunity which is unprecedented will probably be limited. The authorities believe that the case against our clients is very strong and that the investigation has been fair and balanced and open. I have not heard you to say otherwise about the case or the investigation. Therefore, it becomes especially necessary to be prepared for the next phase. Nonetheless, we would like you to know that with my staff here in Riyadh, we are developing a very powerful strategy to contend with the prosecution in court. Let me say that I am hopeful that a significant outcome may eventuate. It would be enough for us to create a shadow of doubt over the indictment for murder, as that would indeed reduce, if not eliminate, the influence of the Australian family in determining the fate of the nurses.

If the nurses are exonerated, through our combined vigorous efforts to examine the evidence (including yours yet to come), especially if an alternative theory of the crime emerges, then the Waiver will not have been needed. But it is best to lay the foundation for such a Waiver on the part of the Gilford family. At the very least we will start the Gilfords' thinking about the issue in a proper perspective that has until now been lacking. I have explained why even a refusal to waive the death penalty can be used to the benefit of our clients.

The time is ripe now in several other respects. Some months have passed for the Gilfords to come to terms with their grief and to have blind rage dissipate. There is less media glare. There has been some opportunity for other leads to develop, casting doubt on the nurses' guilt. We understand that the Gilfords may now have the benefit of some knowledgeable counseling through the Australian authorities and otherwise.

Of course, as explained in the text of the Rationale, asking for a Waiver before the actual trail is not in the normal Western sequence, but then we all recognize that matters are handled differently in Saudi Arabia, but no less justly,

We have now had a full and frank airing of our respective views and of our understanding of the scope of our respective responsibilities. I expect you to retract much of what you have written between 7 and 11 March. The Rationale, after consideration of any precise revisions you wish to suggest, will be released at an appropriate time that will be decided by myself in consultation with the British Ambassador. There is still the need to apply your expertise in examining the evidence, to the extent we are given the opportunity. I recommend, for your own benefit, that you consult with the British Foreign Office, and on that basis continue offering your assistance in matters within your competence. You have a standing invitation to visit Saudi Arabia. I continue to have the highest regard for your professional achievements and standings, and I trust that this view is reciprocated. In that way, notwithstanding this rather unpleasant exchange of your own making, we can resume attending to the best interests of our clients. I have asked Mr. Michael Dark of my law firm, with whom you have been in regular contact and who is very familiar with these matters, to review this letter before dispatch, and he concurs with its contents.

Sincerely yours,
Salah Hejailan

APPENDIX E

Letter to the Sharia court
report written by Salah Hejailan

To: Honourable President and
Members of the Common Suits Council
The Supreme Shari'ah Court
Al-Khobar

From: The Law Firm of Salah Al-Hejailan
On behalf of the two British nurses,
Lucille McLauchlan and Deborah Kim Parry,
Acccused

Your Honours:
It is really a very delicate and serious task which you have been given in this case where there is no evidence before you save the confessions which are covered with a multitude of suspicions and conflicts as shown in the several versions and the obvious conflicts in content that affect their accuracy and their reliability. Also the two accused withdrew their confessions for several reasons of which you were informed in the two first sessions and which were entered into the court record. There is no need to repeat them here.

We are aiming here to reveal all the facts so that you will be well informed before you pass your just judgment. Our presentation will be as follows:

First: In respect of the confessions:
- *It is not true, as some people say, the "confession is the master of evidence or the strongest evidence."*

In our brief of 19/1/1418, we gave our presentation regarding duress, the position of Shari'ah scholars about it and the effect of confessions based on it. We attached the documents that show the particulars of the physical and moral duress to which the two nurses were subjected, as recounted by the nurses. We do not know why it is said that "confession is the master of evidence." Maybe it is that a confession may be superior to other evidence. It is in fact the worst and weakest of evidence for several reasons the most important of which is that it is against the nature of things. It cannot be imagined that a man would give evidence for his own conviction unless he wanted by his declaration of his crime to boast of taking revenge or retaliation for his honour, for the chastity of a woman in his family or because he is mad or mentally disturbed, etc.

Confession is always accompanied by the assumption that it has been taken against the will of the accused. The element of doubt is always there even if it appeared it was taken without pressure or illegitimate influence, because nobody wants to kill himself.

The Shari'ah scholars expanded the concept of duress in its physical and moral aspects. They included promise, threat, violence (irrespective of its degree), pressure in a prolonged interrogation, and every interrogation that was made in a late hour of the night.

If we add to this the mental or psychological sickness of the accused at the time of the interrogation and that the female is more responsive to duress than the male, this will prevent reliance on a confession elicited from such interrogation.

Confession is not the aim of investigation, as some investigators believe. It is the aim to find the facts and no more.

Therefore, the court in its capacity as the legal guardian of rights and individual freedom should undertake to be strict in accepting any confession and exert its utmost care to ensure that the confession is free of defects.

One of the defects stated by the two nurses against the safety of these confessions is the sexual assault. Who can say that the sexual assault is improbable. If it is likely to take place in a society which believes in sexual liberty then it is even more likely to take place in a society which does not permit such sexual liberty and inflicts punishment on the perpetrator. In fact, the person who is naturally and psychologically prepared to commit such sexual assault would not be deterred by punishment, morals or religion.

Therefore, if there is any defect in the confessions as appears from the statements of the two accused given to the court, this argument should be considered fundamental to considering the safety of the confessions.

The established rule in this respect is that one element of evidence should support another. No evidence is sufficient by itself to convince the judge. Confession is no exception to this. The judge should corroborate his reliance on it by other evidence.

Most judicial systems and international conventions prefer to safeguard the rights and freedom of the individual and to avoid committing errors in the very serious field of criminality. Some major states provide in their constitutions that "no one shall be convicted and no criminal punishment shall be inflicted on a person if his confession is the only evidence in the case." Thus, confessions should be corroborated by other evidence, because confessions, as it is said, are the start of the evidence and not the end.

2.   Defects ascribed to the confessions of the two accused:

2.1   A confession not certified by Your Honours—and signed by others—on 13/8/1417 given by Deborah Parry as follows:

- *That the deceased Yvonne Gilford was the one who started the problem on the night of the incident by asking Deborah Parry to practice lesbianism with her. But Deborah refused, became upset and wept until Lucille arrived responding to the telephone call of the deceased to solved their problem. Yvonne was very angry and upset because of the refusal of her request. Then Yvonne asked for the same abnormal act from Lucille who was trying to calm her but Lucille slapped her on the face, causing her to fall, with the subsequent aggravation of the problem that was started by Yvonne. (Please refer to page 7 of Deborah's confession [copy enclosed] dated 13/8/1417, Attachment No. 1).*

- *This is contrary from and different to the confession certified by Your Honours, i.e., Deborah's confession of 13/8/1417, where it is stated at page 2 that the reason for the quarrel and the acute anger of Yvonne and Deborah is that Yvonne (the deceased) informed Deborah that she intended to terminate her sexual relationship with her and that she formed a relationship with another, a fact which made Deborah angry, upset and tearful.*

In the confession referred to in (a) there is evidence that there was no lesbian relationship with either of the two accused and Yvonne because they were very angry with her when she asked them respectively to indulge in the abnormal practice with her. The confession referred to in (b) contains evidence of the existence of this relationship between with Deborah and Yvonne and the intention of Yvonne to terminate it.

If it is admitted that there is a conflict between the confessions they have to be disregarded and set aside, particularly when the matter concerns a vital issue such as the lesbian relationship. It is a vital issue because it was the cause of the quarrel, which resulted in the death as stated in the confessions. We will revert in paragraph 6 to the statements of the victim's family who vehemently denied that the victim was a lesbian. This denial shows in itself the contradiction of the attitude of the victim's brother when he denied this lesbian relationship upon which the confessions were based and which is stated to have been the cause of the anger and of the quarrel.

2.2   One of the contradictions and inconsistencies between the confessions given by the two accused is that one of them states that the victim, Yvonne, initiated the hostility by running to the kitchen, picking up a knife and trying to attack Deborah and Lucille. But they resisted in defense of themselves: the consequence of which was Yvonne's death. (Please refer to page 8 of Deborah's confession dated 13/8/1417 signed by all the investigating authorities and those present and the confessions not certified [copy enclosed]—Attachment No. 2).

Defense of oneself is the act of repelling or driving away the assailant and discharges the person defending himself from responsibility even if his act results in killing in self-defense, i.e., if there was imminent danger to himself or to another, or to property or the chastity of his family or property or chastity of others, it is permitted for this danger to be repelled by killing. A description of the requirements and limitations is in the book of Dr. Abdul Fattah Khedr, "Criminal Law—Its General Provisions in the Contemporary Context and according to Shari'ah Scholars," vol. 1, 1402–1982.

Although this confession is not certified as others, yet it is given by the accused Deborah and signed by the investigators, translators and a member form the Public Morality Authority. There is nothing to prevent reliance on it, assuming the confessions were not made under duress.

2.3   In the confession of Lucille it is stated that she pressed the pillow on the victim's face while Deborah's statement says "we did not suffocate her with the pillow." This agrees with what is sated in the post-mortem report which concluded that the death was the result of stab wounds and not suffocation. (Please refer to page 8 of Deborah's confession referred to in paragraph 2 above, Attachment No. 2.)

A report by another forensic doctor commenting on the forensic report submitted in this case states that if suffocation occurred by a pillow the following traces should appear:

- *Injury to and around the mouth as a result of hard pressure and the resistance of the victim.*
- *Detection of saliva or blood on the pillow.*
- *Existence of petechial hemorrhages in the eyes.*

But as we said the autopsy report did not state them.

In order to destroy the confessions and to disregard them it is suffi- cient that there exists one defect in them represented by inaccuracy of any information in them. What about the several contradictions and incon- sistent matters which are the base for these confessions (e.g. lesbianism) or the absence of responsibility (e.g. self-defense) or the absence of the act altogether (e.g. suffocation with the pillow)?

2.4   One can easily see that the confessions were dictated.

This has recurred in a noticeable way in the confessions of the two accused, giving one the impression that they were dictated by a person who knows the Hegira calendar and the Gregorian calendar. The two accused do not know the Hegira calendar because they are new arrivals in the Kingdom. For only about three months elapsed ever since their arrival in the Kingdom.

This defect is quite apparent in the dates of use of the ATM card as we will mention later.

One who is not accustomed to the use of Hegira calendar will need years in the Kingdom to remember the Hegira calendar and get accus- tomed to its use. It is not possible for the two accused to have mentioned in the said confessions, the Gregorian calendar for past events they remember, with the corresponding Hegira calendar. This is a noticeable defect that throws doubt on the truth and safety of those confessions.

2.5   Furthermore, Your Honours are aware of the weakness, unusu- al pressure, tension and panic suffered by the two accused at the time of their arrest and interrogation for long hours without sleep, and they were brought before Your Honours after midnight to certify their confessions.

If we are aware of the above and add to it the psychological and the nervous weariness of the accused Deborah before her arrest and even before arrival to the Kingdom we would say that her condition had reached a condition of helplessness, lack of any degree of resistance and she had become completely submissive to the least pressure on her. This is clear from the doctor who was treating her and who has recorded her past illness in the attached document (Attachment No. 3). We have already stated that a female is more responsive to duress than a male and to the least pressure or intimidation.

Confessions given under such circumstances cannot be imagined to be safe and relied upon solely. They have to be accompanied by strong evi- dence corroborating them if they are to be relied upon.

The matter is very serious. It relates to murder and serious punishment the effect of which cannot be repaired if an error is made or if certain information is revealed later that would have resulted in an acquittal if known earlier.

History is full of excesses or errors committed by governors and judges. It is probable and in accordance with the nature of men. Perfection is for

God above. Our Prophet (PBUH) who is infallible, feared falling into error in judicial cases presented before Him. He said "I am a human being. You are litigating before me. Maybe one of you is more intelligent in his argument. Thus, I give judgment according to what I hear. If I judged to one anything from the right of his brother, he should not take it, because I am cutting to him a piece of fire." (Narrated by Bukhari and Moslen and Shab Alsunan). When He appointed governors, He declares such fear.

The companions were following the Prophet (PBUH). There is an example of this in the message of Omar bin Alkhattab to Abu Musa Alashari when he was appointed governor of Yemen:

"A judgment which you passed and found upon reconsideration to be unjust should not prevent you from reverting to what is right. To revert to what is right is better than to continue in falsehood."

It is very important here that a case occurred during the reign of Ali bin Abi Taled the Khalifa. An accused confessed to murder before him and corroborated his confession with other evidence. But the surprise was that at the last moment he was found not guilty.

If this happened during the time of Ali, could it not happen with any judges of today?

Third: In respect of guarantees provided for the Kingdom's regulations in all stages of accusations investigations and trial:

In the constitution of Saudi Arabia issued in 1412 (1992) Article 1 states the following:

"Islam is the religion of the state and the Qur'an and the traditions of the Prophet (PBUH) are the constitution of the state."

Article 41 of the same constitution provides that all residents in the Saudi Arabia are subject to its laws and regulations.

Article 26 provides that Moslem Shari'ah protects human rights, equality and justice for all Moslems, non-Moslems and residents who are assured of protection.

If things are so, we have to remember some principles of criminal justice adopted by Moslem Shari'ah. The most important of these principles is the following:

- The principle "man is considered innocent." This principle is supported by Shari'ah and by reason.

God said "Ye who believe! If a wicked person comes to you with any news, ascertain the truth, lest ye harm people unwittingly, and afterwards become full of repentance for what ye have done." (Aljujurat verse 6)

"Ye who believe! Avoid suspicion as much (as possible), for suspicion in some cases is a sin. And spy not on each other nor speak ill of each other behind their backs. Would any of you like to eat the flesh of his dead brother? Nay, ye would abhor it: ...But God for God is oft returning most merciful."

"But they have no knowledge therein. They follow nothing but magic; and magic avails nothing against truth."

There are other verses warning against *"assumption"* and confirming that the rule is that a man is innocent until there is sufficient evidence to the contrary.

The interest of society is realized by putting things in their right place and by achieving the objectives aimed for by Moslem Shari'ah.

The emphasis of this is the saying of our Prophet (PBUH). *"If people are adjudged according to their allegations, then some people allege blood retaliation from others and their property."* But *"oath should be administered by the defendant."* In another narration *"The burden of proof is on the plaintiff and the oath is on the one who denies the allegation"* (narrated by Baihaqi)

- The principle *"To avert hudud: determinate crimes and qisas, retaliation, by suspicion."* (No penalty on suspicion criterion) Suspicion and doubt erases the evidence that covers it. It should be put aside and not to be relied on. In case of doubt in evidence, things should be interpreted in favour of the accused according to (the rule of innocence). A man should remain innocent until he is proved guilty.

If we are now speaking about the guarantees provided by Saudi Regulations according to the Moslem Shari'ah, we have to say that these guarantees are many, some of which are the following:

An accused should not be interrogated hand-cuffed (Article 99 of the Public Security Dept. Ordinance)

A woman can only be interrogated in the presence of a person in a degree of consanguinity precluding marriage or a neutral committee, including at least one member form the Morality Authority to guarantee non-occurrence of anything that is prohibited by Shari'ah (The Ministry of Interior letter no. 16/6838 and dated 26/8/1408 and the Ministry Circular No. 4935 dated 28/11/1409).

The right to have the help of a lawyer in all stages (Article 39 of the Investigation and Prosecution Regulations, Article 19 of the Procedure Regulations before the Grievance Board. Fatwa of the General Mufti of the Saudi Arabia Sheikh Abdulaziz Bin Baz referred to in reference of Moslem fatwa by Sheikh Mohammed Abdul Aziz Al-Musnid vol. 3 p. 505)

The right of the accused to defend himself freely. It is based on God saying *"God orders for justice and charity."*

The duty of the investigator to do his utmost to corroborate the evidence if any (Article 138 of the Public Security Ordinance).

The duty of the investigator to record the accused's statements in the minutes of investigation and not what the investigator believes or suggests (Article 58 of the Investigation and Prosecution Dept. Regulation)

The investigator's duty not to expose the accused to physical or moral duress whatever its degree. The investigation should be by wise means. (According to what is decided by most of the faquhs, a confession elicited by duress is not admissible as indicated in our first brief). (Article 100 of the Public Security Dept. Ordinance and order of the Council of Ministers No. 277/8 dated 22/2/1405 confirmed by order no. 825/8 of 25/4/1402).

Were all these guarantees observed?

Were the two accused interrogated while they were hand-cuffed? Did Your Honour ascertain this and that they attended the trial leg-cuffed in the first and second hearings?

If this was before Your Honour and during the stage of the trial, what was the condition during the investigation to elicit their confessions?

Was the interrogation carried out in the presence of a member from the Morality Authority which presence is mandatory as referred to throughout the stages of interrogation, or was he reported only to have signed the confessions to complete the formality?

To ask the member of the Morality Authority about these confessions is very important, for these confessions will be nullified if it is proved that he did not attend during any part of these confession no matter how small it was.

Did the Investigation Authority safeguard the right of defense freely for this or were they exposed to the treatment they explained during the first and second hearings of the trial?

If the interrogating authorities were careful for providing these guarantees, how did they publish information about it in Al Hayat newspaper (e.g. the statement of the bank manager)—as soon as the two accused were arrested and before the appointment of the lawyer. And the announcement that the scene of the crime was found clean from any traces or evidence such as fingerprints, etc., and other information mentioned in the police minutes of meeting and which were withheld from us in spite of our recurrent demand as indicted. No matter how clean was the scene of the crime, there are modern scientific means to discover the traces.

- *Were the investigators able to ascertain the ownership of the broken chain found thrown on the floor of the bedroom of the victim? This chain will lead to an important information in this case.*

In most murder case, the culprit leaves behind many traces—without his knowledge—no matter how professional he was. Is it imaginable that the crime would be free of any trace? Confession in case when caught red-handed is something, and in other cases another thing. Other evidence can corroborate.

We cannot interpret shopping of the accused before their arrest as evidence against them. This is a mere assumption, because this shopping is a custom for these people in an important occasion called "Christmas." It was natural behavior for the two accused.

To say that they withdrew amounts of money form the bank with the deceased's ATM card is not evidence against them. The two accused have already denied this as shown and as mentioned by Lucille in her diary which was submitted with the first brief with the report of her fiancé (Attachment No. 3). And why were they arrested only after the fourth withdrawal while they were put under control from the time of the commission of the crime with other nurses?

There are several questions and suspicions as indicated.

Your Honour, we are facing a very serious position. God knows the truth. We pray God to lead you in the right way so that no innocent person would be exposed to punishment or a culprit escape punishment.

Conclusion and Summary
Honourable President and Members

Many points were presented earlier about this serious case. Most of them concerned the confessions, both the certified and the uncertified or those approved only by all parties including the member from the Morality Authority. This last—although not presented to you but it is approved as we indicated—is denied by our clients the same as the other confessions certified by Your Honour.

These last confessions which were not presented to Your Honour included—as we indicated—information contradictory to the certified confessions. We have clarified this contradiction before: e.g., the two accused denied suffocating the deceased with the pillow. Lucille denied that she has any knowledge of the bankcard—except from investigators—both accused denied the lesbian relationship and reproached the deceased for her demand and also the attempt of the deceased to attack them with the knife she brought in a state of nervous rage from the kitchen—being reason for self-defense. The confessions included the Gregorian and Higra calendars which show that the confessions are dictated by the investigators, for it is impossible for the two accused who are new arrivals to Saudi Arabia (about three months only) to be familiar with the Gregorian calendar and the corresponding Hegira calendar.

- Our briefs included the most important guarantees provided by the Kingdom's Regulations, our inquiry whether the Investigating authority abided by these guarantees.

We pointed out that according to these guarantees an accused should not be interrogated hand-cuffed. We pointed out this guarantee was violated before Your Honour in the two first hearings where the two accused were brought leg-cuffed. We inquired if this happened before Your

Honour, what about the condition during their interrogation to obtain confessions?

- We emphasized the results by the forensic doctor which agree with the confessions that you did not peruse, for at the end of his report, the forensic doctor stated that death resulted form stab wound and did not find any trace for suffocation of deceased by a pillow as stated in the certified confession. This was denied by Deborah in the confession which you did not peruse although it is approved by the Investigation Committee and a member of the Morality Authority.

- We inquired about the role of the member of the Morality Authority. Did he attend all the interrogations and hear the confessions or did he attend some of them and did not attend others, but he signed them all for the sake of formality as required by Regulation. We concluded by saying that these confessions are nullified if it is proved that the member of the Morality Authority did not attend nor hear any part of confessions—however small— given by the two accused. We demanded Your Honour to ascertain.

We inquired about the previous murder crime that occurred in the Housing Complex and the authorities did not identify the culprit. We requested Your Honour to investigate the circumstances of this incident. May be there are some similarity in the circumstances between the two cases? Particularly we explained the absence of real motive for killing of deceased by these two weak girls in such a vicious way, resulting in twenty-one stab wounds and nine bruises and abrasions i.e., committed in a way that can only be an attack by a savage killer who is highly emotionally motivated to revenge from the deceased. This deep desire can only be generated after long years and bad relationship between the culprit and the victim. This is not present in the case of the accused who arrived in Saudi Arabia for the first time about 3 months before the commission of this crime. Their relationship was not cemented either positively or negatively.

Most of our discussion concentrated on the certified confessions and others because defects were involved in all of them. Confession is the worst of evidence because it is related to the idea of torture or duress and bears contradiction between the desire of the accused to escape punishment and submitting evidence of his conviction. Also, confession may be an appearance of madness or psychological disturbance.

- Our brief stated that the wisdom aimed by Shari'ah is not present in case of the heirs, because they lived all their life in a society that rejected capital punishment and are not affected by hatred to demand retaliation as is the case in Moslem societies.

As to the mother, her present mental sickness renders us facing a suspicion that prevents the brother from claiming qisas.

We could imagine conciliation or pardon form the mother if she is in her sound mental state. This suspicion is sufficient to prevent the brother form clinging to qisas. It is agreed by most of faqihs that—quisas is not divisible. Any person among the heirs may drop it by pardon (Please refer Oudah Book vol. 2 R160)

- We pointed out that precaution should be taken not to rely on confessions only—even if they are not defective. It is better to be corroborated by other evidence.

We referred to the probability of error by investigators, judges and governors and mentioned the certain legal evidence for occurrence of each error. We gave an example from judgments of Ali Bin Abi Taleb.

The rule "to avert hudud" determinate punishments by suspicion is well established in Islamic Fiqh. We also quoted from Aisha in this respect where it said that it is better for the Imam (Governor) to commit error by pardon instead of committing error in punishment.

Concluding we invoke God to lead you in the right way.

Salah Ibrahim Al-Hejailan

ᴀᴘᴘᴇɴᴅɪx F

Travel Information

Saudi Arabian Travel Advisories:

The nurse's case raises a number of questions regarding travel and social conditions within in Saudi Arabia. The following information obtained from the United States Department of State (Saudi Arabia—Consular Information Sheet, June 26, 1998 see: www.travel.state.gov/saudi.html) is offered as a guide to Westerners traveling to Saudi Arabia. Similar information can be obtained from appropriate agencies in other Western nations, or the Saudi Arabian embassy. Travel advisories and other information subject to change.

Entry Requirements:

Passports valid for at least six months and visas are required for entry. Single-entry visas for business and work, to visit close relatives, and for transit and religious visits, but not for tourism, are the only visas available for Americans. Airport visas are not available. Visas are required for persons on vessels calling at the port of Jeddah. All visas require a sponsor, can take several months to process, and must be obtained prior to arrival. Women visitors and residents are required to be met by their sponsor upon arrival.

Residents working in Saudi Arabia generally must surrender their passports while in the Kingdom. The sponsor (normally the employer) obtains a work and residence permit for the employee and for any family members. Family members of those working are not required by law to surrender their passports, though they often do. Residents carry a Saudi residence permit (iqama) for identification in place of their passports. The U.S. Embassy and Consulates General cannot sponsor private American citizens for Saudi visas.

Foreign residents traveling within the Kingdom, even between towns in the same province, carry travel letters issued by employers and authenticated by an Immigration official or a Chamber of Commerce officer. Police at all airports and dozens of roadblocks routinely arrest and imprison violators.

Visitors to Saudi Arabia generally obtain a meningitis vaccination prior to arrival. A medical report is required to obtain a work and residence permit. This includes a medical certification. For further information on entry requirements, travelers may contact the following Saudi government offices in the U.S. at Royal Embassy of Saudi Arabia, 601 New Hampshire Ave., N.W., Washington, D.C. 20037, telephone (202) 333-2740

Saudi Customs, Religious Police, and General Standards of Conduct: Islam pervades all aspects of life in Saudi Arabia. It is the official religion of the country, and public observance of any other religion is forbidden. Non-Muslim religious services are illegal, and public display of non-Islamic religious articles such as crosses and bibles is not permitted. Travel to Makkah (Mecca) and Medina, the cities where the two Holy Mosques of Islam are located, is forbidden to non-Muslims.

The norms for public behavior in Saudi Arabia are extremely conservative, and religious police, known as Mutawwa'iin, are charged with enforcing these standards. Mutawwa'iin, accompanied by uniformed police, have police powers. To ensure that conservative standards of conduct are observed, the Saudi religious police have harassed, accosted or arrested foreigners, including U.S. citizens, for improper dress or other infractions, such as consumption of alcohol or association by a female with a non-relative male. While most incidents have resulted only in inconvenience or embarrassment, the potential exists for an individual to be physically harmed or deported. U.S. citizens who are involved in an incident with the Mutawwa'iin should report the incident to the U.S. Embassy in Riyadh or the U.S. Consulates General in Jeddah or Dhahran.

The Saudi Embassy in Washington , D.C. advises women traveling to Saudi Arabia to dress in a conservative fashion, to wear ankle-length dresses with long sleeves, and not to wear trousers in public. In many areas of Saudi Arabia, particularly Riyadh and the central part of the Kingdom, Mutawwa'iin pressure women to wear a full-length black covering known as an "abaya" and to cover their heads. Most women in these areas, therefore, wear the abaya and carry a headscarf to avoid harass-

ment. Women who appear to be of Arab or Asian origin, especially those presumed to be Muslims, face a greater risk of harassment.

Some Mutawwa'iin try to enforce the rule that men and women who are beyond childhood years may not mingle in public, unless they are family or close relatives. Mutawwa'iin may ask to see proof that a couple is married or related. Women who are arrested for socializing with a man who is not a relative may be charged with prostitution. Women who are not accompanied by a close male relative have not been served at some restaurants, particularly fast-food outlets. In addition, many restaurants no longer have a "family section" in which women are permitted to eat. These restrictions are not always posted, and in some cases women violating this policy have been arrested.

Women are not allowed to drive vehicles nor ride bicycles on public roads. In public, dancing, music, and movies are forbidden. Pornography, which is very broadly defined by Saudi authorities, is strictly forbidden. Homosexual activity is considered to be a criminal offense and those convicted may be sentenced to lashing and/or a prison sentence, or death.

Alcohol and Drugs:

In Saudi Arabia, penalties for the import, manufacture, possession, and consumption of alcohol or illegal drugs are severe. Convicted offenders can expect jail sentences, fines, public flogging, and/or deportation. The penalty for drug trafficking in Saudi Arabia is death. Saudi officials make no exceptions. Customs inspections at ports of entry are thorough.

U.S. citizens are subject to the full force of Saudi law as well as that of any country in which they are traveling or residing. The U.S. Embassy and Consulates General have no standing in Saudi courts to obtain leniency for an American convicted of alcohol or drug offenses.

Besides alcohol products and illicit drugs, Saudi Arabia also prohibits the import, use, or possession of any item that is held to be contrary to the tenets of Islam. This includes non-Islamic religious materials, pork products, and pornography. Saudi customs and postal officials widely define what is contrary to Islam, and therefore prohibited. Christmas decorations, fashion magazines, and "suggestive" videos may be confiscated and the owner subject to other penalties and fines. The private ownership of weapons is prohibited. Imported and domestic audiovisual media and reading matter are censored.

Traffic and Road Safety:

Traffic accidents are a significant hazard in Saudi Arabia. Driving habits are generally poor, and accidents involving vehicles driven by minors are not uncommon. In the event of a traffic accident resulting in personal injury, all persons involved (if not in the hospital) may be taken to the local police station. Drivers are likely to be held for several days until responsibility is determined and any reparations paid. In many cases, all drivers are held in custody, regardless of fault. Those involved in an accident should immediately contact their sponsor and the U.S. Embassy or nearest consulate.

Health Conditions and Medical Facilities:
Malaria is endemic to the low-lying coastal plains of southwest Saudi Arabia, primarily in the Jizan region extending up the coast to the rural area surrounding Jeddah. Visitors to the region are advised to take precautions to avoid being bitten by mosquitoes. As a further precaution, all persons intending to travel to this region should seek medical advice regarding recommendations for prophylactic anti-malarial medications. Basic modern medical care and medicines are available in several hospitals and health centers in Saudi Arabia. Doctors and hospitals often expect immediate cash payment for health services. U.S. medical insurance is not always valid outside the United States. The Medicare/Medicaid program does not provide for payment of medical services outside the United States. Supplemental medical insurance with specific overseas coverage, including provision for medical evacuation, has proven to be useful. For further information, travelers can contact the Centers for Disease Control and Prevention's international travelers hotline, telephone 1-888-232-3228, their fax service at 1-888-232-3299, or their Internet site at http://www.cdc.gov.

Information on Crime:
Crime is generally not a problem for travelers in Saudi Arabia. However, private Saudi citizens who perceive that conservative standards of conduct are not being observed by a foreigner may harass, pursue, or assault the person. The loss or theft of a U.S. passport abroad should be reported immediately to local police and the nearest U.S. embassy or consulate. Useful information on safeguarding valuables and protecting personal security while traveling abroad is provided in the Department of State pamphlet A Safe Trip Abroad. General information about travel to Saudi Arabia can be found in the Department of State publication Tips for Travelers to the Middle East and North Africa. Both pamphlets are available from the Superintendent of Documents, U.S. Government Printing Office, Washington, D.C. 20402.

Sources Consulted

Books:
Anderson, J.D. , 1975, Islamic Law in the Modern World. Greenwood Press, Publishers, Westport, Connecticut
Dawood, N.J., 1990, The Koran, Penguin Books Ltd., London
Khan, M.A., 1996, Islamic Jurisprudence, Avon Books, London
McLauchlan, Lucille, 1998, Trial by Ordeal, Mainstream Publications, Edinburgh, Scotland)
O'Connell, Mick, 1999, Mercy, Harper-Collins, New York

Newspaper Articles:
Boggan, S., Stabbing, suffocation and blood money: final act of a drama fit, Independent, pp 2, May 20, 1998
Davies, C., Freed nurses fly home to storm over selling stories, The Daily Telegraph, May 21, 1998
Esmaeili, H. & Gans, Jeremy, Cultures Colliding in Court. The Australian, 1997
Haddad, Y. Y., Islam, The Canadian Encyclopedia, McClelland & Stewart, Inc., September 6, 1997
Ibrahim, D. & Agencies, British nurses appear at Alkhobar court, Arab News. p. 5, May 19, 1997
Shears, R. , Nurses' freedom hope, Lawyer claims victim's brother may have no right to call for blood, Daily Mail, p. 23., June 11, 1997
Shears, R., Let her killers die says former lover of murdered Nurse, Daily Mail, p. 24, September 6, 1997
Shehan, C., New pressure on dead nurse's brother, Sydney Morning Herald, p.16, June 10, 1997
Smith, H., Saudi Arabia to free two British nurses—ambassador, Reuters. News Service, May 19, 1998
Horsburgh, Susan, A grieving brother could decide whether Saudi Arabia beheads two British nurses, justice: the power of life and death, Time International, pp. 65, August 8, 1997
Walmsley, D., I'm glad my husband's killer was beheaded: David Walmsley talks to the widow of a Briton stabbed to death in Saudi, The Daily Telegraph, September 25, 1997

Journal Articles
Butti, Sultan and Butti, Ali Al-Muhairi, Islamisation and Modernization Within the UAE Penal Code Law: Shari'a in the Pre-Modern Period, Arab Law Quarterly, 1995
Souryal, S.S., The religionization of a society: the continuing application of Shariah law in Saudi Arabia. Journal for the Scientific Study of Religion, Vol. 26, No.4, pp. 429-449, 1987

Souryal, S. & Potts, Dennis, The penalty of hand amputation for theft in Islamic justice, Journal of Criminal Justice. Vol.22, No. 3, 249-265, 1994

Duncan, Mary Carter, Playing by Their Rules: The Death Penalty and Foreigners in Saudi Arabia, The Georgia Journal of International and Comparative Law, Vol. 27, Fall, 1998

Additional Sources

BBC News UK: Saudi nurses in hiding, BBC Online Network, May 21, 1998

BBC News UK: Convicted British nurse has depression, BBC Online Network, January 11, 1998

BBC News UK: Saudi nurse defends new job, BBC Online Network, September 18, 1998

Combined News Services (May 22, 1998): British nurse tells of Saudi torture/says murder confession forced, Newsday, Inc., pp. A18

Interviews

Salah Al-Hejailan August 22, 1998
Robert Thoms, August 22, 1998
Michael Dark, March 22, 1999
Jonathan Ashbee, April 3, 1999
Rodger Pannone, April 6, 1999
Fares Hejailan, April 7, 1999